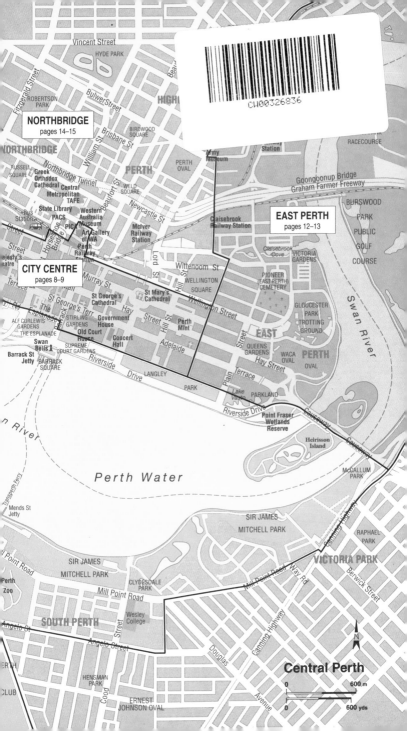

PERTH

smart guide

Part of the Langenscheidt Publishing Group

Contents

Areas

A–Z

Below: a team from the Surf
Life Saving Club hits the water.

Left: the towers of Perth's city centre rise above Kings Park.

Atlas

Below: an impressive collection of didgeridoos.

3

Perth

It is Australia's most isolated state capital, on the world's most isolated continent. It is no wonder, then, that Perth has a strong sense of cheerful indifference towards the activities of the rest of Australia. Perth prides itself on the sparkling waters off the coast, its laid-back locals and a lifestyle that is centred around getting out into the natural beauties that surround the city.

Perth Facts and Figures

Population: 2 million in Western Australia, 1.55 million in Perth greater metropolitan area
Indigenous population: 2 percent
Population born overseas: 42 percent
Area: 5,386 sq km (2,080 sq miles)
Population density: 280 people per sq km (725 per sq mile)
Language: **English**, but around 25 percent speak another language at home
Distance from London: 14,000km (8,700 miles), with an approximate flying time of 17 hours and 30 minutes
Locals' top activity: 'eating out at a restaurant'
Nickname: 'sandgropers', for an unusual insect found in WA

The Most Remote Capital

Perth is a paradox: a state capital city that still feels like a holiday town. Isolated by the bush, ocean, desert and rolling agricultural land, it remains the most remote state capital in the world. Its special appeal as a city lies in the fact that it is a place where a big-city sophistication combines with small-town friendliness. And of course, it has some spectacular natural splendours on its doorstep, with kilometres of golden beaches and good proximity to the rolling green lands of the Swan Valley. Perth is located on the west coast of Western Australia, the country's largest state, which brings in the majority of the nation's GDP thanks to its wealth of natural resources, in spite of much of the state being uninhabited and home only to scrubby bush.

Captain James Stirling founded the City of Perth as part of the Swan River colony in 1829. Although the territory was claimed by Britain, explorers from countries such as Holland and France had been visiting WA since the early 1600s, and the land had been the home of indigenous people for around 50,000 years. The colony officially lasted until 1832, and Perth trundled along until the 1890s, when the discovery of gold turned Perth into a city. Riches from the Kalgoorlie goldfields paid for hundreds of public buildings as the government of the day struggled to cope with the tide of newcomers.

Looking to the Future

Perth today is an affluent, prosperous city. Though the goldfields have been exploited, the nickel, iron and gas resources found in Western Australia are fuelling another boom and new expansion, drawing skilled migrants from around the world and regenerating the inner city with tourism-driven ventures, new homes and commercial towers. With the influx of new residents and the cultures that they bring, Perth is becoming ever more cosmopolitan as its population continues to rise. By 2010 the city will have even more glass-and-steel towers, entertainment and leisure centres on the

Below: outside Council House, bronze sculptures of a recognisable Australian icon.

river, revitalised public buildings and cultural centres occupying former industrial sites. Key to Perth's new look is the Northbridge Link, a scheme to sink the railway line that has long dissected the city. The expectation is that once it is completed, it will make a huge difference to the 'people-friendly' factor of the city. There are also plans for a major redevelopment of the Swan River frontage on which the city of Perth is perched, which remains an unused and beautiful stretch of river.

The People of Perth

Locals enjoy a fairly relaxed lifestyle by world standards. With excellent year-round weather, there is a strong emphasis on the outdoors.

Enjoying free time at weekends often centres around taking advantage of getting outside, whether that's taking the dog to the beach, the kids to a local park or catching up with friends over a Sunday afternoon beer at a favourite pub. While having a good time is high on any local's list, locals are keen to be a part of the state's prosperity, and working hard, before hitting the beach, is the norm. Meanwhile, many workers have been taking advantage of the current minerals boom in the north of the state and moving. This is causing frequent staff shortages, especially as tourism rises; visitors are increasingly discovering the sunny charms of this laid-back city that knows how to enjoy the good life it has made for itself.

Highlights

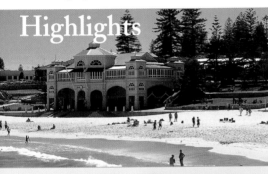

▲ **Cottesloe Beach** Great for swimming, lazing on golden sands and watching glorious sunsets over the Indian Ocean.
▶ **City views from Kings Park** Get a bird's-eye view of the city and the sprawling Swan River.

▶ **Café culture in Fremantle** Spend some time watching the world go by on Fremantle's 'cappuccino strip'.

▲ **Station Street Markets** Covered markets offering an incredible spread of exotic produce and a lively atmosphere.

▲ **Swan Valley wineries** Sample world-class wines at the Swan Valley's cellar doors.
▶ **Aussie Rules football** Head to an Eagles or Dockers game along with sports-mad locals throughout winter.

Swan River
and Kings Park

The Swan River and Kings Park are synonymous with Perth. The Swan River curls around the edge of the Central Business District (CBD) and extends its arms through suburbs, heading south to Fremantle and east to the Swan Valley. The river is an integral part of the city's culture, giving locals a place to walk, cycle, boat, play and fish. Kings Park is perched above the Swan River and overlooks the CBD, offering locals an inner-city retreat filled with walkways, spectacular views and rare flora.

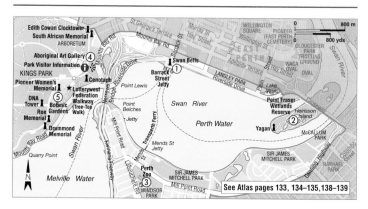

See Atlas pages 133, 134–135, 138–139

The Waterfront

The waterfront south of the city centre focuses on **Barrack Street Jetty** and the **Swan Bells** ①. Immense copper sails cup a green-glass bell tower *(see box, right)*. The bells, a gift from the church of St Martin-in-the-Fields in London, were installed in the bell tower to mark Australia's bicentenary in 1988. They rang in the New Year in London for 275 years and have proclaimed the coronation of every British monarch from George II in 1727. There's a small charge to see the bells and take the lift to the outside observation level, which has great views of Perth.

The jetty is the departure point for various river cruises to Fremantle and up to the wineries in the Swan Valley, as well as the ferry to South Perth. There are a few coffee and food options on the jetty, ranging from 'pay what you can afford' Hare Krishna cuisine at Annalakshmi, to fine dining on the waterfront at **Halo**. If you take some time out to ponder the world here, you may even see some dolphins flit past.

Walking with your back to the river up Barrack Street will take you to St Georges Terrace. This is the heart of the business area *(see p.8)*, where folk in suits rush around trying not to get blown over by the winds that can funnel down the terrace. Modern office towers rub elbows with colonial buildings, and the two are not hard to confuse.

SEE ALSO RESTAURANTS, P.101; TRANSPORT, P.121

Heirisson Island

The walk from Barrack Street Jetty to **Heirisson Island** ②, which is bisected by the Causeway, can be done comfortably in half an hour. A small colony of Western Grey kangaroos are housed in an enclosure here; move quietly around the track and you may be able to spot them grazing. At the southern tip of the island there is a bronze statue of Yagan, an Aboriginal leader killed in 1833.

Named for a French sailor, François Heirisson,

Left: the Swan Bells.

SEE ALSO CHILDREN, P.38;
TRANSPORT, P.121

Kings Park

No other city in the world has such a large area of natural bushland at its heart. The cultivated gardens with lawns, terraces and water gardens are substantial, but form only a small part of the 400-hectare (988-acre) site, which is mainly native bush. Park Visitor Information offers free half-day bush and wild-flower walks conducted by volunteer guides. The park is full of memorials, for example, commemorating those lost in two world wars, the Boer War and the Bali bombing of 2002.

Along Fraser Avenue there is a choice of eateries with river views. On the river side of Fraser Avenue, the **Aboriginal Art Gallery** ④ sells fine indigenous arts and crafts. It usually has an Aboriginal artist in residence.

Beyond the Cenotaph at the end of Fraser Avenue is the spot to come for that panoramic river or city view. Here you will find the heavily planted **Botanic Gardens** ⑤. By keeping to the path, with the Swan on your left, you will come to a spectacular Tree-Top Walk with views across the river.

SEE ALSO ABORIGINAL CULTURE, P.27; PARKS, P.89–91

who rowed a longboat upriver to the island from his moored ship *Le Naturaliste*, Heirsson Island has been a site of political controversy. In 1984, an Aboriginal camp lasted for 40 days before its occupants, land-rights protesters, were evicted. Today, however, it is more commonly used for open-air concerts than protests.

SEE ALSO PARKS, P.88–9

Below: walking in Kings Park.

The South Bank

Over the Causeway, riverside parkland leads back downriver, with a café, boat ramp and boat hire at Coode Street. At Mends Street, the Transperth ferry departs for Barrack Street every half-hour during the day, and every 15 minutes at peak commuting times. Mends Street has several eating options, and the **Perth Zoo** ③ is also a short stroll from this junction, along Labouchere Road.

When the zoo opened in 1897, six keepers looked after two lions and a tiger. Now there are 1,800 animals and 120 staff. One of the highlights is the Australian Bushwalk through recreations of different Australian ecosystems, including a tropical rainforest. There are no fences in this section, so you can get up close with kangaroos and other native fauna.

When visiting the Swan Bell Tower, take note of the impressive copper sails which enclose the glass tower. In the 1980s 1- and 2-cent coins were phased out of circulation, as inflation had rendered them virtually worthless. Many of these copper coins have been melted down and used as the copper in the bell tower's sails.

City Centre

Perth's city centre is made up of a short stretch of skyscrapers and office blocks, with older buildings and shopping offered to the north of St Georges Terrace. Recent economic boom times have seen office space in Perth stretch to its absolute limit, making it the tightest market in Australia. With the Swan River on one side of the city and Kings Park bordering another, it is a small, concentrated area of commerce and retail, with very few locals actually living in the city's jurisdiction. With new licensing laws, small bars are gradually opening up, adding to the nightlife, but most of the action in the city centre takes place during waking hours.

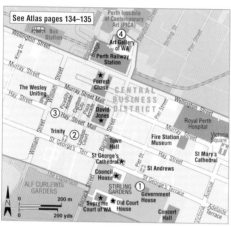

See Atlas pages 134–135

Perth is a city on the move. There are plans to link North-bridge and the city to make the two areas blend smoothly into one another, as currently there is no pleasant way to walk between them, while the foreshore is also due a large Sydney Harbour-style redevelopment, as is the link between the city and South Perth. Depending when you visit, you'll notice varying degrees of construction.

The CBD

The Central Business District converges upon the grid of streets north of Barrack Street Jetty. St Georges Terrace, Hay Street and Murray Street run east–west, with King Street, William Street and Barrack Street running north–south. Most offices are located on St Georges Terrace, with the bulk of retail happening on Hay, Murray and King streets.

Historic Perth

When Perth city centre was redeveloped, many historical buildings were demolished. However, the best place to see those that survived is **St Georges Terrace**, Perth's first thoroughfare, stretching the length of the CBD and centring on **Stirling Gardens**, where a collection of buildings date back to the founding of Perth.

Along the terrace you'll see the **Old Court House**, built in 1836. It is still in place, next door to **Government House** ①, the residence of the state governor, to the rear of Stirling Gardens. The Old Court House shares the gardens with the Supreme Court of WA (1903). It was here that the first settlers pitched their tents in 1829. Alongside the gardens is **Council House**,

Left: the towers of the CBD.

Left: shoppers in the Murray Street Mall.

tral area between Wellington Street and the **Murray Street Mall**. The **Myer** department store complex also forms part of Forrest Chase.
SEE ALSO SHOPPING, P.108–9

Cultural Perth

Perth's cultural centre lies north of the railway tracks, joining the CBD with Northbridge; it is most easily accessed via the walkway over Wellington Street from Forrest Chase shopping mall. On the city centre side, the **Art Gallery of Western Australia** ④ is the main building to the right after you cross into the centre, its slab-sided face generally advertising its latest exhibition. Inside, several floors of modern, well-lit galleries display more than 1,000 works of art, including Australian and international several significant Australian artists, including Arthur Streeton, Frederick McCubbin and Brett Whitely. There is also a large Aboriginal art gallery and regular, free public tours.
SEE ALSO MUSEUMS AND GALLERIES, P.76–7

Below: sculpture in the grounds of the Art Gallery of WA.

the modern headquarters of Perth City Council. Nearby **St George's Cathedral** was begun in 1879 when times were hard, and completed in 1888, four years before the Western Australia gold rush.

West along St Georges Terrace from here is **London Court** ②, one of only a few major building projects dating from the years of depression in the 1930s. The mock-Tudor ambience is enhanced by its narrow alley, bijou shops and decorative porticoes at each end, one in Hay Street Mall and the other on St Georges Terrace, the latter topped by a St George and the Dragon clock. Of all the city centre's arcades, this is the one to comb for Australiana (think koala badges, emu-leather handbags, kangaroo-fur coin purses), jewellery and other gifts.
SEE ALSO PARKS, P.91; SHOPPING, P.108

The Shopping Centre

King Street, on the west end of the grid, was once dubbed 'the Paris end of Perth'. While no doubt this was originally just a nice spot of marketing, the moniker has stuck. While you have to squint to see Paris in King Street, it is without a doubt the stylish end of town. Big-name luxury brands make themselves at home next to über-cool clothing and shoe shops, as well as several cafés.

A warren of shopping malls and arcades lies between St Georges Terrace and Wellington Street, each with its own individual character. **Hay Street Mall** ③ is home to many retailers, including national department store group **David Jones**, where you'll find some of Australia's best fashion designers, a gourmet food hall and lots more.

You'll also find plenty of shops in Forrest Chase, a cen-

Leederville

Located a couple of minutes' drive from the city of Perth, Leederville is the place to come if you seek a relaxed inner-city vibe. The district has a distinctly European-influenced air, with excellent delis and other eateries packing the streets. Indeed, other than eating, the main activity in Leederville is people-watching, usually from a sidewalk table at one of the myriad cafés dotted along the Oxford Street strip. The suburb has a laid-back, urban feel, with cool kids with facial piercings making themselves at home next to young families having coffee with the family dog by their side. Hip boutiques and popular pubs round out the bohemian vibe.

The History of Leederville

The Leederville area was initially founded by private settlers William Leeder and John Monger. Between 1850 and 1868 Perth experienced rapid growth, with 10,000 convicts arriving. With the added pressure on food, Leederville's wetlands areas were primarily used as market gardens, and dairy and poultry farms.

After World War II, migration policy was changed and a large number of European migrants arrived in Perth. Many of these settled in the Leederville and North Perth areas, drawn to the cheap land and large amounts of market-garden space. Today the market gardens have well and truly disappeared, and Leederville is one of the trendy suburbs of Perth, located only 4km (2.5 miles) from the city centre.

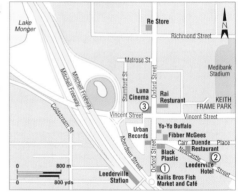

Oxford Street

Heading up Oxford Street immediately gives you a sense of what Leederville is all about. The large Continental European migrant population that settled in Leederville many years ago, well before the suburb was remotely

trendy, has ensured that the culture is centred around food, relaxing with friends over a coffee and watching the world go by.

On the main part of Oxford Street you'll walk past the large **Kailis Bros Fish Market** ①. The Kailis family originally came from Greece, and now their seafood business is just about the largest in WA, supplying restaurants, cafés and supermarkets. They have a large fresh seafood and café outlet in Leederville. Continuing your culinary journey along Oxford Street, you will find more cafés per square centimetre than it seems any-

Left: fresh fish at Kaili's.

lian and Vietnamese foods being just a sample of those on offer. There are a few interesting shops and boutiques worth a look, too, often reflecting the quirky nature of the suburb.

The main action on Oxford Street ends at the Vincent Street intersection. On one of the intersection's corners is the Art Deco-style building of the **Luna Cinema** ③. Red carpet and a big staircase set the mood; the main theatre is a grand example of the architecture and is a great place to escape the summer heat. The Luna shows films that you won't find at the big complexes, and in the summer runs an outdoor cinema next door, where punters can bring a picnic and a bottle of wine and enjoy a film from a deck-chair in the warm night air.

If you continue up Oxford Street away from the central buzz, you'll quickly come across popular Italian deli, **The Re Store**. The smells of cured meats, exceptional cheese and yeasty bread hit you instantly and are only the start of things on offer here. If you can speak Italian you'll be fussed over even more.
SEE ALSO FILM, P.57; FOOD AND DRINK, P.61

one could reasonably need. However, it can be surprisingly difficult to get a table on a Sunday morning, when locals flock to the street to read the papers and sip on a latte, while also doing battle with lycra-clad cyclists who descend on the strip in bright gear, with bikes in tow.

The **Leederville Hotel** ② now occupies one of Leederville's oldest buildings. Built in 1897, the two-storey building's architect remains unknown. Extensive alterations and additions were made in the 1920s and 60s. On the corner of Oxford and Vincent is the old post office, built in 1897. Now a café, it still retains its original character and terracotta Marseilles-patterned tiled roof.
SEE ALSO FOOD AND DRINK, P.60–1; PUBS AND BARS, P.96–7; RESTAURANTS, P.102

Lake Monger

A short stroll west along Vincent Street, crossing under the freeway overpass, will take you to Lake Monger. Prior to white settlement of the area, Lake Monger was known as Galup to the land's indigenous people, the Nyungar. Galup was a site used by Aborigines for camping, hunting and fishing. Today Lake Monger is home to a large group of black swans – WA's state emblem. You can stroll around the 3.5km- (2.2 mile-) lake, or just take a shorter walk through the bird habitat area on purpose-built boardwalks.

The lake is surrounded by weeping willows and other lovely trees, and on one side there is a children's playground. The track around the lake is popular with walkers, joggers and cyclists.

Eating and Entertainment

Cuisines from around the world are well represented, with Spanish, French, Malay, Indonesian, Turkish, Mongo-

Once a year Oxford Street is shut off to cars and a leg of the Perth Criterium series is held here. The best cyclists in town descend on Oxford Street and race in a series of heart-in-your-throat laps at top speeds. Sometimes there are spectacular crashes as bikes and riders go akimbo, but there is always great action as well as a fantastic vibe. It usually happens over the Australia Day long weekend in late January.

East Perth

East Perth is becoming a spectacular gateway to the city, a riverside precinct for living and socialising that is taking shape out of a former industrial wasteland. Its main area, Riverside, is set to develop further over the next decade, but the rebuilding of East Perth that began in the early 1990s is already a sight to see. The central Royal Street and Plain Street are where you'll find the buzzing centre of shops, cafés and restaurants. When redevelopment started in the early 1990s, state government allocated one percent of the cost of landscape and architectural projects to public art. The results are dotted along the banks of the inlet and throughout the district.

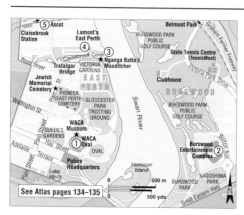

See Atlas pages 134–135

A short walk up Plain Street off Royal Street is where you'll find the colony's earliest link with its own history. Two new town houses on Plain Street have unique back gardens. Peer through their iron gates, and you'll find the Jewish Memorial Cemetery. The houses are built over the original Hebrew burial grounds that opened in 1867. About 30 people were buried here before a new cemetery opened for people of all faiths in 1899.

Arriving in East Perth

The deck of a boat on the Swan River is the place to stand and take a first look at East Perth. Cruisers from Barrack Street Jetty motor past the north bank, where the slender, light towers of the **Western Australian Cricket Association** (WACA) ① ground are prominent. Closer to the foreshore and its pilot wetlands area are the heritage-listed police headquarters, and behind the WACA is **Gloucester Park** harness-racing track.

Boats sail under the Causeway, passing Heirisson Island before sighting the distinctive, pyramid-shaped **Burswood Enter-**tainment Complex ② on the south bank.

SEE ALSO NIGHTLIFE, P.84; SPORTS, P.113; TRANSPORT, P.121

Around Claisebrook Cove

The best of East Perth, however, is yet to come, on a northerly diversion off the Swan and into **Claisebrook Cove** ③, a stream of fresh water found and named by Captain Stirling in his 1827 exploration of the river. He called it Clause Creek, after the ship's surgeon, Clause, which later evolved into Claisebrook.

Leisure grounds at the mouth of the inlet give way to houses and apartments, with restaurants and cafés fringing the waterway. A footbridge, Trafalgar Bridge, crosses Claisebrook, and footpaths and cycle paths run around it. One of Perth's best restaurants, **Lamont's East Perth** ④, looks over the water to Burswood. Cruise boats can go no further along the waterway, but you can proceed on foot. The elimination of motor traffic and the encouragement of walking and bike-riding is part of the East Perth ethos.

An interesting architectural mix is a vital element of the new East Perth. Influences range from oriental, Regency and traditional European to concrete and steel, with a broad spectrum of materials and colours to

toughest test of stayers in Australia.

Perth's **Burswood Casino** can also be found here, as part of the Burswood Entertainment Complex. It is also home to two hotels, many restaurants, a public golf course and the permanently inflated **Dome**, which is host to concerts and sporting events such as the annual Hopman Cup tennis tournament in January.

The casino offers all the usual gambling options of course, such as blackjack, roulette, baccarat, pai gow, poker, Caribbean stud and craps 24 hours a day, except Christmas Day, Good Friday and Anzac Day.

SEE ALSO NIGHTLIFE, P.84; SPORTS, P.113–114, 115

match that diversity. This is inner-city living with style. Everyone has a veranda, patio or terrace, but there is no space for private gardens. This makes public parks like Victoria Gardens, with its free barbecues and picnic tables under the trees, and **Queen's Gardens**, landscaped with lily ponds and English trees, all the busier.

Like so much of Perth, Claisebrook is an ancient area with powerful Aboriginal links. This river-bank area is known as **Nganga Batta's Mooditcher** (Sunshine's Living Strength) and is a 'place of hope and friendship' for Aboriginal people. The standing stones on the foreshore form a winding trail, the **Illa Kurri Sacred Dreaming Path**, which describes the chain of lakes and wetlands spanning the land before Perth was built.

SEE ALSO RESTAURANTS, P.103

Racing and the Casino

Watching horse-racing is very popular in Australia, and **Ascot** ⑤, with its grand 1900s buildings and grandstand, is WA's principal racecourse, used for summer racing (in winter the action moves to nearby **Belmont Park** at Goodwood Parade, Burswood). Ascot's 300m (330yd) inclining straight is regarded by experts as the

Below: the towers of the WACA grounds.

Cricket

There are few better places to experience the national sport in all its forms than the grounds of the WACA, WA's governing cricket body founded in 1885. More than 40 days of first-class cricket are played each summer season (Oct–Mar) ranging through international one-day matches, Test matches and inter-state contests. The WACA provides special shuttles on match days, running to the ground from the Entertainment Centre car park in Wellington Street, via the train and bus stations; regular bus services to Nelson Crescent include the free red CAT bus.

Even if there isn't a match to watch, you may want to visit the WACA's Museum, where you can discover more about the history of the club and many of the great international cricketers.

SEE ALSO SPORTS, P.113

13

Northbridge

Cut off from the city centre by the Perth–Fremantle railway, Northbridge, an old and distinctive neighbourhood packed with heritage-listed buildings, has evolved separately from the CBD, even though it is just a short hop away over the Horseshoe Bridge. During the day, Northbridge is the place to come for sourcing interesting European and Asian foods at bargain prices, while at weekends it turns into Perth's night-time hot spot. Clubs, bars, pubs and restaurants heave into the wee small hours as people dance, eat and drink the weekend away. A thriving cultural life rounds out the area and ensures its place as one of Perth's most interesting districts.

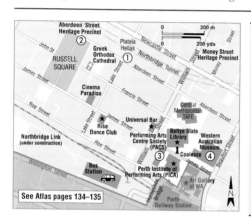

See Atlas pages 134–135

The '**Northbridge Link**' is a redevelopment plan which will reunite Northbridge with the city centre by submerging part of the railway and linking King Street on the south with Northbridge's Lake Street in a continuous stream of galleries, cafés and entertainments. One of the most important elements of the project is a new entertainment and sports stadium. The work was originally due for completion in 2009, but the project has been slowed and is still a few years off being complete.

Northbridge's Culture and Heritage

The longest-established communities of Perth, after the Aborigines and the British, are Mediterranean Europeans, who began arriving in WA after World War II. The dome of the **Greek Orthodox Cathedral** in Russell Square is a striking symbol of the time. The next significant wave of immigrants was Asian, and the little Chinatown at the east end of James and Roe Streets shows its influence.

A Mediterranean atmosphere prevails in Northbridge on long summer evenings. The area is ideal for strolling in the early evening, alfresco dining, and dawdling as you watch the passing parade. The intersection of Lake and James streets, the hub of the entertainment district, is a good place to linger over a drink and take Northbridge's pulse. Almost every restaurant makes use of the pavement, and on a warm evening they're all bustling.

A more recent feature that represents the area's culture are the distinctive polished-concrete pillars of **Plateia Hellas** ① on Lake Street, meaning 'Greece Town Square', a meeting place for the community in Northbridge. Named in tribute to the area's Greek population, the feature is considered the jewel in the crown of Northbridge's redevelopment.

Meanwhile, the **Aberdeen Street Heritage Precinct** ② contains nine buildings that have been retained due to their heritage, streetscape and economic value.
SEE ALSO WALKS AND VIEWS, P.123–5

Contemporary Arts

WA's creative-arts scene centres on the end of Lake Street, near the WA Art Gallery, where the CBD joins with Northbridge. Here you'll find the **Performing Arts Centre Society** (PACS) ③, occupying a former school. The soaring main gallery has studios on a mezzanine, and there's a bar-cum-café and a performance theatre on the ground floor.

Left: enjoying a few beers at the Brass Monkey pub.

paintings. The oldest life-fossil known is displayed here, which was discovered in 1999 in the Pilbara region. The museum has a pleasant coffee shop next to the **Old Gaol**, built by convicts in 1855–6 and now crammed with memorabilia of Perth life since James Stirling's expedition of 1829, including a complete original courtroom, a pedal radio that kept outback families in touch, and a complete pharmacy from 1917.

SEE ALSO CHILDREN, P.38–9; MUSEUMS AND GALLERIES, P.77–8

A Nightlife Hub

Northbridge is known as *the* place to head out on a Friday or Saturday night. Much of the action focuses on the bar and club scene, which keeps going until the small hours. A range of tastes is catered for, from funk and jazz at the **Universal Bar** to serious dance tunes at **Rise**. However, if finding your way past boozy young things isn't your scene, perhaps go for dinner at one of the many restaurants and head home before things start to get messy around midnight. Northbridge has also been known for violence on these nights, but there is a strong police presence, and you generally won't find much trouble.

SEE ALSO MUSIC AND DANCE, P.81; NIGHTLIFE, P.85

Sharing space with PACS are the **Photographers Gallery**, **WA Actors Centre** and **Impressions Gallery**, which shows prints. **Artrage**, Perth's alternative arts coordinator, is around the corner.

The newest attraction at PACS is the **Blue Room**, where around 20 shows a year are put on by the writers, directors, actors, technicians and managers who create them. Each shows runs for a two- to three-week season.

Across the concourse, the **Battye State Library** contains the state archives, film and photographs. The main attraction for casual visitors is likely to be the discard bookshop in the front lobby.

The black-and-white sculpture *Coalesce*, by Akio Makigawa, in front of the library, has become a popular meeting place; the stepped forms symbolise the stages of acquiring knowledge.

SEE ALSO THEATRE, P.116

The Western Australian Museum

Next to the Battye building is the **Western Australian Museum** ④, an elegant red-brick and sandstone building with a colonnaded upper floor. In WA, scientists have access to some of the oldest land on Earth and its earliest life forms, not to mention evidence of the life of early man, such as rock

Below: investigate fossils at the Western Australian Museum.

Each March, Northbridge and the City of Perth have City Food and Wine Month. You'll find some great offers on at cafés and restaurants, as well as having the chance to attend cooking demonstrations, farmers' markets and masterclasses. *See Festivals and Events, p.55.*

Subiaco

Subiaco is a suburb that has it all, cool shops, top restaurants, great culture, major sports grounds and a lively vibe. Creative industries such as advertising, publishing and design tend to be based here, and housing prices certainly indicate that Subiaco is one of the most desirable addresses in Perth. Much of the residential architecture is cottage-style, or bungalows, but many original homes have been restored and extended, and make for impressive viewing. As a visitor, Saturday lunch or brunch can be combined with a look around the ever-popular Station Street Markets and some upmarket shopping or a visit to the theatre.

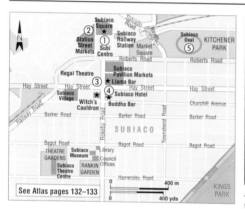

Above: boutique-hopping in trendy Subiaco.

On the Ground

Subiaco Station was sunk below ground in 1998 in a daring piece of planning designed to create the spectacular **Subi Centro** ①, a complex of houses, apartments and offices that has transformed the area.

From the top of Rokeby Road, it is a 15-minute walk to the Saw Avenue entrance to Kings Park, which has 400 hectares (1,000 acres) of natural bush, as well as lakes, lawns, children's playgrounds and botanical gardens. Walking is easy, but bicycles can be hired for longer explorations from a kiosk in the Fraser Avenue car park.

To rejuvenate the north, the rail line had to go. The process of sinking it through the 1990s was complex and controversial, but what the America's Cup did for Fremantle, Subi Centro has done for Subiaco. Drab, empty factories were replaced by smart apartments, offices and restaurants. The station square is spotless, and the electric trains, unseen, glide noiselessly in and out. For WA the concept of creating a new urban space by pushing the rail underground was revolutionary.

Markets and Theatres

On the western side of Subiaco Square are **Station Street Markets** ②. This covered market is a Perth institution that has somehow survived the gentrification all around. Locals come here every weekend for the big spread of exotic fruit and vegetables produced by local Asian family businesses. In addition, home-made and natural organic produce, art and crafts are spread across 100 colourful stalls.

The hub of Subiaco lies at the Rokeby/Hay crossroads. The Subiaco Hotel faces the **Regal Theatre** ③, neighbours since the 1930s. The Regal opened as a 'hard-top' cinema in 1938, replacing the open-air Coliseum Picture Garden, one of many in its time. While many Subiaco

Left: bountiful produce on offer at the Station Street Markets.

are interspersed with several notable and popular restaurants, such as **The Witch's Cauldron**, **Star Anise** and **Bistro Felix**.
SEE ALSO RESTAURANTS, P.105–6

Football Fans

Subiaco is also home to the **Subiaco Oval** ⑤, WA's headquarters of AFL (Australian Football League), otherwise known as Aussie Rules, the unique Australian game. The Oval is also the home base and grand final venue for the Western Australian Football League, as well as being the home ground of local WAFL side, simply called 'Subiaco'.

In the long winter season there is an AFL match every week, plus WAFL matches at the Oval and elsewhere around Perth. A striking example of sporting architecture, the Oval has all-seater modern stands with a capacity of 43,000. The AFL teams in Perth are the West Coast Eagles (who have won the premiership several times) and the Fremantle Dockers (who align themselves as a 'working-class' side, although their fans are usually anything but). You'll know if a game is being played, as the roar of the crowd can be heard kilometres away.
SEE ALSO SPORTS, P.112

theatres closed down, the trend was reversed at the Regal, where live performance replaced film in 1977.

The interior of the Regal is as stunning as the Art Deco exterior. The original chrome-and-jarrah fittings are still in place, as is Paddy's Bar (and his chair), named after Paddy Baker, who bought the cinema in 1946. Paddy also installed the love seat in the balcony, as well as the 'Crying Room', so that mothers could attend to their offspring while still watching the show. Paddy died in 1986, leaving his beloved building to the people of WA. The Regal is now listed with the National Trust.

Also on the Rokeby/Hay crossroads is the **Subiaco Hotel** ④, which has been transformed from a standard pub into a cosmopolitan

entertainment spot, with an award-winning restaurant.
The Llama Bar (opposite the Regal) is owned by the same proprietors and hits the same high standards.
SEE ALSO FOOD AND DRINK, P.61; PUBS AND BARS, P.98; RESTAURANTS, P.106; SHOPPING, P.109; THEATRE P.117

Consumer Society

At the last count Subiaco had over 100 cafés and restaurants, homeware stores, health and beauty outlets, jewellery stores and book-stores. Stylish shops

Right: colourful buildings line Subiaco's streets.

Fremantle

The port city of Fremantle, which lies 19km (11.8 miles) from Perth, is an intriguing mix. Known as a laid-back place, where long-standing hippies rub shoulders with young up-and-comers, Fremantle has become a residence of choice since it hosted the America's Cup in the 1980s and hit the map. Now, property prices are soaring in this former working-class, artists' enclave; the main drag is even known as 'the cappuccino strip', where everyone heads for a pavement seat to spot and be spotted. Watch boy racers cruising past, while locals walk their organic fruit and vegetables home from the markets and visitors soak up the relaxed atmosphere.

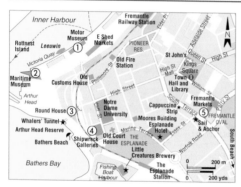

Formula One champion Allan Jones's world-beating Williams, more than 50 motor-cycles, and the Aston Martin V8 Volante used by James Bond in *The Living Daylights*.

At the far end of the quay you will see the modern, sail-like roof of the **Maritime Museum** ②, an imaginatively executed exploration of Fremantle's many and varied maritime industries. Even if maritime exhibits are not of interest to you, it is worth a visit just to admire the exceptional architecture.

A short walk from Victoria Quay is Arthur Head, site of the **Round House** ③. This is WA's oldest public building and its first gaol, built in 1830 where Captain Fremantle landed to claim Western Australia for the British Crown. WA's prison populace soon

About Fremantle

Freo, as it is known locally, has a friendly, confident feel and a Mediterranean flavour. Artists have thrived in Fremantle for years, with generations of writers, actors, painters, musicians and crafts workers finding inspiration and low-cost studios in the old port buildings. Artists were initially drawn to the area as it was away from the busy, business-focused attitude of Perth, and even now, living in Fremantle can get you labelled as a 'Freo hippie', a dig aimed at the port city's laid-back style. Now, of course, to own property in Freo, you would have to be a very well-heeled hippie.

Fremantle Port is WA's main port, and shifts an enormous amount of cargo each week, yet is noticeably clean, with colourful mountains of containers and gantries. Even the distant oil-storage tanks look scrubbed white and silver. Day and night, cargo containers waiting clearance to enter and unload linger off the coast near Rottnest Island.

Around the Quay

The quay is also a departure point for the ferry to **Rottnest Island**, as well as the location for the main maritime sights and the **Motor Museum** ①. Based on Peter Briggs's family collection, its exhibits include world land-speed record-breakers, such as historic racing cars, including

Right: relaxing on 'the cappuccino strip'.

output is sold around the state and widely exported.

North of the brewery and boatyards, a host of restaurants, ice-cream parlours and cafés line the Fishing Boat Harbour, a working harbour for a 500-strong fleet. From here, head up Essex Street which leads to South Terrace, known as **'the cappuccino strip'**. Along with good coffee, you'll also find some of the best beer. The **Sail and Anchor** boutique pub brewery serves many excellent brews.

First opened as a market hall in 1897 and now splendidly restored, **Fremantle Markets** ⑤ is National Trust-listed. Spread across more than 150 stalls you'll find fresh fish and crustaceans, fruit and vegetables, cheeses, freshly baked bread, coffees, herbs, spices and health foods. Crafts and Australiana also abound: sheepskin and leather goods, jarrah and cane products, dried wild flowers, opals, local shells and pottery are all here.

SEE ALSO FOOD AND DRINK, P.60; HOTELS, P.71; PUBS AND BARS, P.98; SHOPPING, P.109

outgrew the capacity of the Round House and its eight small cells. A series of bigger prisons replaced it, but the Round House was used as a police lock-up until 1900.

Below the jail is **Whalers' Tunnel**, which was cut through the rock in 1837 to connect Bathers Beach and the jetty with the settlement. Hunters of the Fremantle Whaling Company used the tunnel to drag their kill through, and it is the only remnant of the whaling industry

that was so crucial to the young colony.

From here, walk along Cliff Street (right off the High Street). At the end of Cliff is the original WA Maritime Museum, now known as the **Shipwreck Galleries** ④, devoted to marine archaeology. Treasures from the *Batavia*, a famous Dutch shipwreck, are on display alongside relics from other ancient wrecks.

SEE ALSO EXCURSIONS, P.46–8; MUSEUMS AND GALLERIES, P.78–9

The Esplanade and the Main Drag

From the Shipwreck Galleries, proceed along Marine Terrace to reach the prominent **Esplanade Hotel**. Modern extensions are well blended into the original facade, built in gold-rush 1890s style like many Fremantle hotels. One of the main attractions here is the harbourside **Little Creatures Brewery** (also a bar and restaurant), whose

If you visit South Beach (at the end of South Terrace) you will notice a statue out in the water. It depicts the famous WA engineer C.Y. O'Connor, who designed the port of Fremantle and also the pipeline responsible for taking water out to Kalgoorlie and the goldfields. Sadly for C.Y., he suffered so much abuse over the pipeline that he rode his horse out from South Beach and shot himself. The pipeline was completed after his death and is considered an engineering masterpiece.

Cottesloe, Claremont, Swanbourne and Scarborough

The Perth area is blessed with some beautiful coastline, and there are multiple choices when it comes to where to visit. Scarborough has one of the best metro surf breaks, while Swanbourne is great if you want a full body tan without bather marks. Meanwhile, the western suburbs of Cottesloe and Claremont are home to some of Perth's most fabulous folk.

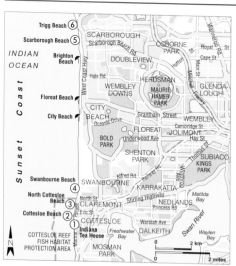

For the ultimate Perth 'Sunday session' head to the **Ocean Beach Hotel** (OBH). Perched across the road from Cottesloe Beach, the OBH attracts a young crowd, often from the country. In hot weather the large windows are opened, and you can enjoy getting tan while you drink beer and watch the sun set. Also legendary for its Sunday drinking session is the Cottesloe Hotel, where, if you miss out on prime real estate near the front of the bar, you can enjoy the party atmosphere in the rear courtyard. See also *Pubs and Bars, p.99.*

Cottesloe

Cottesloe is a trendy beach-side suburb, boasting some of Australia's most spectacular views and highest property prices. A million dollars won't get you much of a house here, but using the beautiful beaches and hanging out is free, and locals do it in droves. It is equally popular with visitors, who come to soak up the cosmopolitan vibe.

Dominating the beachfront is the graceful outline of the **Indiana Tea House** ①, an elegant, colonial-style restaurant housed in a wooden pavilion right on the beach, the perfect place for a sundowner as the sun sets over the Indian Ocean. The bars and cafés that line Marine Parade are set slightly back from the water, but they enjoy great ocean views and fling open their windows to let patrons make the most of them. On a hot summer's day the lively atmosphere floats out onto the street.

Cottesloe Beach ② is great for swimming, especially in the summer, when surfing is banned except beyond the groyne. Landscaped lawns rise up behind the beach, lined with Norfolk pines, whose distinctive shape helps lend Cottesloe its character and provide sunbathers with some much-needed shade.

If the crowds become too much, **North Cottesloe Beach** ③ is far quieter, and only a minute's drive along Marine Parade or a short walk along the beach away from Cottesloe. There are no facilities and the beach is unpatrolled, but consequently much more peaceful.

SEE ALSO BEACHES, P.28, 29–30; RESTAURANTS, P.107

Left: wine and good food at The Blue Duck, Cottesloe *(see Cafés, p.35)*.

Swanbourne Beach backs onto the SAS (Special Air Service) army base. There is a firing range which is often used, so if you hear the cracks of gunfire, don't panic, it is just the SAS practising their aim.

racks, you soon hit the start of the West Coast Highway, from which several beautiful beaches can be accessed, including **City Beach**, **Floreat Beach** and **Brighton Beach**.

Scarborough Beach ⑤ is the most developed of the beaches in the Perth area. Offering a wide range of waterfront accommodation, it's a popular choice for holidaymakers who prefer to base themselves outside the city centre, as well as very popular with surfers taking advantage of the great breaks on offer.

The beachfront jogging track is always in use by keep-fit fanatics, while for those who prefer a more sedate pace there's the Scarborough Beach to Trigg Beach Heritage Walk. **Trigg Beach** ⑥ offers similar amenities to Cottesloe and is popular with those looking for a few drinks and a bit of rowdiness on a Sunday afternoon.
SEE ALSO BEACHES, P.28–31

Claremont

Claremont is a neighbouring suburb to Cottesloe, minus the beach frontage but with Swan River access. Claremont is known for its stylish shopping options on Bayview Terrace and St Quentin's Avenue, where you'll find Perth's wealthy spending their free time and cash and cruising in expensive cars.

Several Australian designers have stores on the exclusive Bayview Terrace strip; you'll also find the fabulous Mecca, **Zomp** shoes and Witchery for reasonably priced, fashionable women's clothing. In the Bayview Terrace shopping centre (linked from the terrace by Old Theatre Lane) you'll also find the immensely popular **Country Road** clothing and homewear. When you tire of shopping, there are several great eating options on the terrace too.
SEE ALSO FASHION, P.52–3

Swanbourne to Scarborough

North of Cottesloe is **Swanbourne Beach** ④, which is best-known for its nudist bathing on the far side of the dunes. Being situated right next to a military base and accessed by a no-through road, it has plenty of privacy, but swimming conditions can be rough.

Following the road around the back of the army bar-

Right: surfing is very popular at Perth's beaches.

Swan Valley and the Perth Hills

The Swan Valley and Perth Hills are just short drives from the city centre, yet once there, you feel as if you are miles away and, in some cases, that you have stepped back in time. It is one of Perth's perks that it is a small enough city to enable easy access to the distinctive Australian landscape around. Both the Swan Valley and the Perth Hills areas have wonderful villages with great atmospheres, plentiful bushland and lots of fine food and wine to tempt you away from the big smoke.

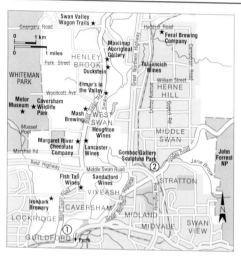

A sweet one is the **Margaret River Chocolate Company**, near **Lancaster Wines**. It sells all kinds of delicious confections, such as hand-made truffles, hot drinks, sauces, cakes, novelties and chocolate bars, and it also offers free chocolate-tastings.

Swan Valley Wagon Trails transports visitors in pioneer-style covered wagons, drawn by Clydesdale horses, through the olive groves and pine forests of the region. Tours vary and can be tailor-made for vineyard tours, evening trips and to meet wine cruises from Perth.
SEE ALSO WINE COUNTRY, P.126–7

The Swan Valley

If there is only time for one out-of-town visit, a trip to **Guildford** ① is arguably the one to make. It is only 30 minutes away by train or road from the CBD, and a further five minutes by car will take you through the vineyards of WA's oldest wine area, where wineries, breweries, restaurants and tourist attractions welcome visitors through the year.

Guildford is easily explored on foot. Close to the train station, the Visitor Centre can provide a map of short walking trails taking from 20 minutes to an hour. Opposite the station, a parade of antiques shops line James Street between the enormous Federation-style **Guildford Hotel** from around 1900 and the Art Deco **Town Hall**.

Sweet Treats

With a number of excellent wineries lining the Swan Valley region, visitors often concentrate their tour on comparing as many wines as possible, but along the trail are dozens more attractions.

German Brews

On the gastronomic trail of West Swan Road, a pair of German-style microbreweries, **Elmar's in the Valley** and **Duckstein**, each make their beer according to the 'Bavarian Purity Law' of

A few kilometres along the Great Eastern Highway is the road to **Mundaring Weir**, which *(see picture, right)* is an impressive sight, even though it is nowhere near capacity due to years of drought. You can walk across the weir, and there is a museum on site.

Left: the Guildford Hotel.

In September it's time for Spring in the Valley. Held across a weekend, wineries are the focus for visitors to the valley. You will see bus-loads of cheerful folk tasting wines, and probably not spitting them out often enough. It is a fun weekend, however, and worth visiting the valley during this time.

about 7km (4 miles) from Guildford.
SEE ALSO PARKS, P.93–4

Kalamunda

At neighbouring **Kalamunda** ⑤, early European settlement of the region can be explored at the **History Village**. It has an original post office dating from 1901, the district's first state school, a settler's cottage, workshops and two railway stations, all equipped with original artefacts and furnishings.

Kalamunda is also the starting point for another round of wineries, in the **Bickley Valley**. Elevated conditions on the Darling Scarp have produced a cluster of award-winning boutique vineyards, such as **Piesse Brook** and Hainault.

1516. Only pure water, malt and hops are used. Other breweries include Feral Brewing Co., Ironbark Brewery and Mash Brewing. Good food can also be found at most of the breweries.
SEE ALSO PUBS AND BARS, P.99

Arts and Crafts

Several wineries have galleries, but the best selection of paintings, sculpture and souvenirs are sold in specialist galleries such as **Gomboc**.

Below: Mundaring Weir.

Gallery Sculpture Park ② in Middle Swan, the southern hemisphere's largest gallery, much of it devoted to outdoor sculpture. Another is the **Maalinup Aboriginal Gallery**. Operated by local Nyungar people, it also offers evening entertainments, storytelling, didgeridoo-playing and bush food-tastings.

Into the Perth Hills

Driving in WA is easygoing, even in the Swan Valley with all its tourist attractions. Driving through the hills of the **Darling Range** is more leisurely still. Like the growing number of commuters living on the semi-rural fringes of Perth, visitors can enjoy speedy access to small towns such as Kalamunda and Jarrahdale, and natural attractions such as **Mundaring Weir** ③ and **John Forrest National Park** ④. Entrances lie along the Great Eastern Highway,

A–Z

In the following section Perth's attractions and services are organised by theme, under alphabetical headings. Items that link to another theme are cross-referenced. All sights that fall within the atlas section at the end of the book are given a page number and grid reference.

Aboriginal Culture

Perth's Aboriginal peoples suffered displacement for years after European settlement, like much of Australia's indigenous population, and it is only recently that some ground has begun to be made up. In 2008, the newly elected prime minister, Kevin Rudd, made a national public apology to the Stolen Generation. There are many sites of recognised profound significance to Aboriginal people in Perth, and increasingly, the Noongar history and culture is being given a voice in the city's museums and galleries.

Perth's Indigenous History

Perth's indigenous population, now known collectively as **Noongar** (also spelt Nyungar) people, belong to the south-west corner of Western Australia. Before the Europeans arrived in 1829, they were divided into 13 separate tribes. They obeyed the mythical laws of the Dreaming, a philosophy that closely connected them to the land.

When white settlers arrived, tribal numbers were decimated by disease and bloody confrontations with the Europeans, including the 1834 'Battle of Pinjarra'. Although the Europeans had initially traded amicably with Noongar people, rifts developed when local tribes were declared as British subjects and sacred land was seized.

As more and more land in the region was turned over to farming, most Aboriginal people were forced into towns or camps. From 1890 to 1958, the Native Welfare Act removed children of indigenous descent from their biological parents, especially children of mixed European and Aboriginal descent. Many Noongar children became part of this 'Stolen Generation' after being forcibly removed from their homes and placed in camps at Carrolup and Moore River. It is estimated that up to 25 percent of Noongar children were sent to these concentration camps.

In the latter decades of the 20th century, past wrongs such as these began to be recognised. Pressure to recognise Aboriginal land rights mounted, culminating in 1992, with the High Court Mabo ruling, acknowledging Aboriginal rights to some traditional lands. This was ratified a year later with the Native Title Act, which has resulted in many long and tortuous claims passing through the courts. Meanwhile the book and film *Rabbit-Proof Fence*, based on the true story of three girls who escaped from an Aboriginal camp during the 1930s, garnered international acclaim and attention.
SEE ALSO FILM, P.56

Rottnest Island

In 1839, Rottnest Island became a penal establishment for indigenous people. Over 3,700 men and boys, most of them Noongar, were imprisoned there for offences such as burning bush or digging up vegetables on their own land. There are believed to be at least 369 indigenous people buried on Rottnest Island. In 1904 the prison was closed, and in 1917 the island was declared an A-Class Reserve, ensuring land could not be leased or sold.

The island is known as 'Wadjemup' to Aboriginals, and has great spiritual significance to them. Following the appearance of a dead whale on a Rottnest beach in December 2005, Aboriginal

Right: Aboriginal artworks.

Left: Noongar Aboriginals celebrate their native land title win in 2006.

One of Australia's top Aboriginal theatre companies is based in Perth. **Yirra Yaakin**, meaning 'stand tall' in the Noongar language, began with a youth theatre project in 1993 and has grown into an impressive, award-winning theatre company. They focus on not only creating important theatre, but also keeping Aboriginal performing arts determined by Aboriginal people. If you can catch a play while you are in Perth, it is worth it. *(See Theatre, p.117).*

elders believe the island is slowly reawakening after its dark years as a prison.

Walking tours, run by knowledgeable volunteer guides, depart daily from the island's Visitor Centre. They cover a range of subjects from Aboriginal history on the island to environmental issues (most are free; some have a small charge).

Aboriginal Art

Aboriginal Art Gallery
Fraser Avenue, Kings Park; daily 9am–5.30pm; Mon–Fri 10.30am–4.30pm, Sat–Sun 11am–4pm; free; bus: 103, 102, 24; map p.133 D1
Sells fine indigenous arts and crafts. It usually has an Aboriginal artist in residence and has a lookout point above.

The Art Gallery of WA
Perth Cultural Centre, 47 James Street; tel: 08-9492 6600; www.artgallery.wa.gov.au; daily 10am–5pm; free; train: Perth City; map p.134 B3
On the first floor of the main building, two galleries house one of the continent's best collections of Aboriginal art, comprised of paintings, bark paintings and carvings giving a comprehensive overview of traditional and contemporary works from Arnhemland, the Central Desert and Western Australia.
SEE ALSO MUSEUMS AND GALLERIES, P.76–7

Indigenart, at the Mossenson Galleries
115 Hay Street, Subiaco; tel: 08-9388 2899; www.indigenart.com.au; Mon–Fri 10am–5pm, Sat 11am–4pm; free; train: Subiaco; map p.135 D1
Indigenart represents a wide range of Aboriginal artists from around Australia, and the quality of work is very high.

Japingka Gallery
47 High Street, Fremantle; tel: 08-9335 8265; www.japinga.com.au; Mon–Fri 10am–

5.30pm, Sat 10am–5pm, Sun noon–5pm; free; train: Fremantle
Specialises in paintings and limited-edition prints by Aboriginal artists, with exhibitions of the works of specific artists and communities changing every six weeks. Contemporary Aboriginal artists of all styles and major Australian regions feature. The ground-floor gallery includes paintings, prints, works on paper, didgeridoos, books and artefacts, and an exclusive range of hand-tufted pure-wool rugs with designs by Jimmy Pike and Doris Gingingara.

Tours

Aboriginal Sites in Kings Park
Kings Park; book through WA Visitor Centre, tel: 08-9483 1111; daily 1.30pm; admission charge; bus: 37, 39; map p.134 A2
Run by a man called Greg Nannup, the tours last for 90 minutes and start daily from the front lawn of Aspects of Kings Park, opposite the State War Memorial on Fraser Avenue.

27

Beaches

Western Australians are proud of their coastline, and rightly so. In a state dominated by dry deserts, the sparkling waters of the Indian Ocean exert an almost hypnotic appeal. For locals, whether gathering with friends for a picnic or taking an early morning constitutional along the shore, the beach is a focal point, especially in summer. It can be hard to tell when one beach has turned into another, as they all merge seamlessly into one, but there are signposts in every parking spot, identifying the beach, the surf and swimming conditions and what facilities are available, invaluable if you are visiting an unpatrolled stretch.

Brighton Beach

Train: Clarkson, then bus: 400

Brighton Beach is a good-sized stretch of sand, framed by attractively landscaped picnic and playground areas. Access is just a short walk from the large car park through the dunes. Lifeguards are on patrol, surfers have their own designated area indicated by blue-and-white signs, and there is a kiosk for refreshments. Primarily, Brighton is a good alternative for those who prefer to be near the attractions and amenities of Scarborough, but without the crowds.

City Beach

Bus: 84

Situated about 12km (7.4 miles) from Perth, City Beach is the name of a suburb as well as the beach. A large grassy area slopes gently down to a wide stretch of sand overlooked by the Surf Life Saving Club. Toilets, a kiosk serving refreshments, and gas barbecue facilities mean you can spend a day here quite comfortably, morning until late. There are also volleyball nets on the sand and a playground for the kids. Parking is plentiful.

Cottesloe Beach

www.cottesloebeach.com; bus: 102; train: Cottesloe

Trains run out to Cottesloe from the city centre. To get to the beach from the station, cross over the railway line, head down Jarrad Street and turn right onto Marine Parade. If you want to investigate Cottesloe's small shopping strip on Napoleon Street, it's

Left: getting the boats out at Leighton Beach.

Left: using sun protection is essential in Australia.

In the height of summer, the sun is exceptionally fierce. To avoid sunburn, visit the beach early in the morning, and try not to spend too much time in the sun. Sunscreen, hats and sunglasses are essential. Most people, unprotected, will start to burn in less than 15 minutes. A burn from the Australian sun is like no other, and you can expect a lot of pain, a lot of heat and possibly peeling and even blistering. If you want the bronzed look, a good spray tan is the smart option. Beauty salons all around Perth can help out.

easy to spy from the train station. Head in the opposite direction to the beach.

Most of the beach action you'll also find several cafés which are happy to take in sandy-footed customers, as well as a surfshop, where you can hire surfboards and purchase clothing and thongs (flip-flops, the essential Australian footwear).

Most of the beach action takes place on the sand in front of the **Indiana Tea House**, as this is where the lifeguards keep a watchful eye. Swimming conditions are generally good here, and surfboards are banned during the height of summer (Oct–Mar), so swimmers have the water to themselves. Surfing is allowed on the artificial reef on the other side of the groyne. Lots of families come here, as there are toilets, picnic benches, barbecues, a children's playground and plenty of room for children to run around. At night, make the most of the floodlit beach and enjoy fish and chips down on the sand.

SEE ALSO RESTAURANTS, P.107

Floreat Beach

Bus: 84, 91

In the lovely, affluent suburb of the same name is a large, attractive beach that is particularly popular with locals. It is patrolled only part-time, so be sure to look out for the red-and-yellow flags. There is a good range of amenities, including toilets, plenty of parking, free public volleyball courts, and a café, kiosk and large children's playground set under brightly coloured shades on a grassed picnic area.

North Cottesloe Beach

Bus: 102 to Forrest Street; train: Cottesloe

North Cottesloe is quieter than the main beach, yet is only a few hundred metres away. There are no facilities and limited roadside parking, but you could leave your car at Cottesloe and walk. The beach is unpatrolled, so you

Below: the sundial at Cottesloe Beach.

Left: at a beachside café in Cottesloe.

Perhaps the premier coastal beach destination in the Perth area, Scarborough is certainly the largest and most developed. Many accommodations have been erected in the area for holidaymakers who prefer to be near the beach, while prime breakers on this part of the coast mean it is a focal point for local surfers. The beach is patrolled, and regular surf life-saving competitions and displays are held here, making for entertaining viewing.

All types of water sports are available, including kite-surfing and windsurfing, or you can just sit back and watch the fun from the grassed picnic area behind the dunes.

It can be hard to know which beach to choose, especially when they merge into one long swath. The following guidelines should help.

For families:
Cottesloe, Mettam's Pool, Hamersley Pool, Hillary's Boat Harbour.

For water sports:
Scarborough and Trigg are best for surfing, and Leighton and Port Beach for parasailing, windsurfing and kite-surfing.

For snorkelling/diving:
Marmion Marine Park (join an organised trip from Hillary's Boat Harbour).

For the best après beach:
Cottesloe and Scarborough.

For nudists:
Swanbourne, north of Cottesloe, has a strip for nudists near the dunes at the northern end.

For rock pools:
Bennion Beach, Watermans Beach.

For dogs:
Whitfords Beach, north of Hillary's, has a dog beach (and an area for horses), with a dog-wash service at weekends. Port and Leighton are good, too.

swim at your own risk. In a prime location overlooking the water is **The Blue Duck**, with balcony views out to **Rottnest Island**.
SEE ALSO CAFÉS, P.35; EXCURSIONS, P.46–8

Port Beach and Leighton Beach

Bus: 103 to Queen Victoria Street

Port and Leighton run into each other. Strong winds pretty much rule out sunbathing, and a sign warns swimmers of strong currents and submerged rocks at Port, but this is a good spot to watch parasailing. Home of the Fremantle Surf Life Saving Club, Leighton Beach is also best-suited to wind- and kite-surfing, as strong currents and submerged rocks make swimming risky. There is a small car park and a kiosk. It is a very popular beach for dog-walking, too.

Scarborough Beach

Train: Glendalough, then bus: 400 to Scarborough

Sorrento Beach and Hillary's Boat Harbour

Train: Greenwood, then bus: 456 to Hillary's Boat Harbour

With plenty of beachside accommodation and the shops, cafés and attractions of Hillary's Boat Harbour right next door, Sorrento is a good place to come for the day. Should you tire of the wide expanse of sand and sparkling ocean, you can easily walk across the car park to Hillary's for a bite to eat or a browse among the shops. Sorrento itself has a beachside kiosk and toilets, and is patrolled by lifesavers, as winds can sometimes make conditions rough.

Locals with very small children should avoid the surf beaches and go instead to Hillary's Boat Harbour. Despite its name, boats are actually prohibited in some parts of the marina, allowing for safe swimming in the flat calm of the harbour. The small man-made beach is always busy with families, many of whom turn up early and set up camp for the day under one of the brightly coloured canvases that provide shade here. There's an adventure playground on the sand itself, while further back from the beach is a small funfair, water slides, mini-golf and trampolines. The beach is patrolled, although conditions are so tame that residents bring their children here for summer swimming lessons.

The surrounding precinct is filled with boutiques, souvenir shops, bars and restaurants, most of which line the timber boardwalk known as Sorrento Quay.

South Beach

Train: Fremantle, then walk 100m/yds south to Phillimore Street, take the CAT bus to South Terrace, then walk 700m/yds to South Beach

You will cross a train track and see a large grassed area before you see the water. South Beach is the southernmost beach in the Perth area. Owing to its proximity to the popular suburb of Fremantle, it often gets overlooked, as most people come to Fremantle to shop in the markets or catch a ferry to Rottnest Island, not to swim. However, South Beach is a real find, and is also a stop on Fremantle's free CAT bus as it loops around town. There is a small café, barbecue facilities, toilets, children's playground, good parking and a grassy area for games.

South Cottesloe

Bus: 102; train: Mosman Park
South Cottesloe Beach has a children's playground on a grassed area set back from

the beach, but is otherwise lacking in amenities. All the facilities of Cottesloe, however, are a stone's throw away, so if you like to lose the crowds but not venture too far from facilities, this is a good spot. Access to the beach is again by steps only, although you can walk back along the sand to Cottesloe itself.

Swanbourne

Bus: 102, stop after North Street
North of Cottesloe is Swanbourne Beach, which is best-known for its nudist bathing on the far side of the dunes. Situated right next to a military base and accessed by a no-through road, it has plenty of privacy, but swimming conditions can be rough. However, if Swanbourne Beach is your top pick, you probably are there for the sunbathing rather than the swimming. There are toilets and lots of parking.

Trigg Beach

Train: Glendalough, then bus: 408 to Scarborough, then bus: 458 to Karrinyup Road
Trigg Beach is another popular spot with surfers and sailboarders. The beach is patrolled, but strong rips often develop which can make swimming dangerous, so it is the place for those proficient in the water. As at Cottesloe, there's a good choice of bars, cafés and restaurants, and a supermarket just a short walk from the beach. On Sundays the bars can get a little rowdy as the legendary 'Sunday session' kicks off in the late afternoon, so if you're not up for partying, it's best to stay away. Clarko Reserve, a big grassed area back from the beach, has picnic tables, barbecues and a children's playground.

Watermans Beach

Train: Warwick, then bus 423 to Cliff Street
Watermans boasts a good stretch of sand and interesting rock pools to explore. The water is calm in the shallows, making it good for children and inexperienced swimmers, and there's a children's playground next to the beach under the shade of the Norfolk pines.

Below: surfing and sailing in the sparkling seas.

31

Cafés

It sometimes appears that no one in Perth actually has a job, as the cafés here always appear to be full, no matter what day of the week or what time of day it is. Relaxing at a café at the weekend with the paper, family and dog in tow is a popular pastime, as is the local activity of people-watching, most common in areas such as Fremantle, Leederville and the city centre. Coffee in Perth is taken very seriously, and the food served also tends to be fresh and of good quality, although prices can vary dramatically. For further listings of places to eat, see *Pubs and Bars, p.96–9*, and *Restaurants, p.100–107*.

Swan River and Kings Park

Old Brewery Café Restaurant

173 Mounts Bay Road, Crawley; tel: 08-9211 8999; daily 7.30am–late; bus: 102; map p.137 D4

Enjoy Swan River views and a crafted beer from the on-site microbrewery. There are plenty of interesting dishes on the menu, such as cumin-spiced lamb cutlets, beetroot couscous and tahini mayo. The venue is flexible, so you could enjoy a three-course meal or just a light breakfast and coffee followed by a stroll along the river banks.

City Centre

Bar One

Lower level, QV1 building, 250 St Georges Terrace; tel: 08-9481 8400; www.bar1.com.au; Mon–Fri 7am–late; train: Perth; map p.133 E2

This funky bar-cum-café attracts people at all times of day. You can pop in for a coffee and have a bite to eat, a more serious pasta lunch, or relax over drinks with a group of friends at the end of the

day. It is popular on Friday nights with young professionals, so if you don't want shoulder-to-shoulder action choose another night to visit. There is a large wine list and excellent mixed drinks. The food is Italian-influenced.

Cino to Go

36a King Street, Perth; tel: 08-9322 1002; Mon–Fri 6.30am–6pm, Sat 8am–5pm, Sun 10am–4pm; train: Perth map 134 A2

This is a local chain serving some of the city's best coffee and light food, such as muffins, coconut bread and fruit salad for breakfast and salads and paninis for lunch, with a range of individual cakes on offer all day. Service is upbeat, and during the week you'll find Perth's most fashionable shooting the breeze out front. Also at: 136 Oxford Street, Leederville; daily 6.30am–10pm

Etro

49 King Street; tel: 08-9481 1148; daily 7am–5pm, Fri dinner from 6pm; bus: red CAT; map p.134 A2

In good weather you will always find Etro's footpath

seating jammed with trendy young things sipping strong coffees. Inside you can enjoy well-priced cooked breakfasts and a large range of tasty lunches and dinners.

Matsuri

Lower level, QV1 building, 250 St Georges Terrace; tel: 08-9322 7737; Mon–Fri noon–2.30pm, daily 6–10pm; bus: red CAT; map p.133 E2

A great spot for a fast and tasty Japanese meal that won't break the bank. Entrées such as the beef tataki are good to share, and the set menus (choice of mains such as ginger fish or chicken teriyaki, plus miso soup, rice and salad) offer good value.

> Most cafés and restaurants in Perth take last orders for dinner around 9pm, so even when people say they are open 'late' this often means orders will be taken and then you are welcome to stay as long as you like after that. If you are keen for a late sitting, make sure you call ahead and ask what time the kitchen closes. If in doubt, book a table on popular nights.

Left: Perth's cafés often run from a proper Aussie breakfast, complete with vegemite and local paper, to light bites at sundown (**bottom right**).

counter, plus a cabinet of treats such as goat's-cheese tarts, salmon roulade and home-baked cakes.

Northbridge

Il Padrino
198 William Street; tel: 08-9227 9065; Tue–Fri 11am–late, Sat 5pm–late; bus: blue CAT; map p.134 A3

The walls of this pizzeria tell its story: everyone who is anyone has acknowledged just how good Nunzio's pizzas are. The Pizza Association of Sicily has even declared him the best pizza-maker in the world.

The Red Teapot
413 William Street; tel: 08-9228 1981; Tue–Fri noon–2.30pm, Sat–Sun dinner from 6pm; bus: blue CAT; map p.134 B4

Small and funky, serving great Hong Kong-style Chinese. There are a few signature dishes, including honey king prawns and salt-and-chilli squid. Booking advised.

Soto Espresso
507 Beaufort Street; tel: 08-9227 7686; Mon–Sun 7am–late; bus: 21

Soto Espresso serves light meals and breakfasts throughout the day until 3pm. The tomato and feta on toast is a tasty bargain.

The quality is excellent for the price. It's flavoursome, generous, and you can BYO.

Taka's Kitchen
397 Murray Street (in Shafto Lane); tel: 08-9324 1234; Mon–Sat 11am–9pm; bus: blue CAT; map p.134 A2

You'll fight to get a table at this popular, cheap Japanese café at lunchtime. With an emphasis on speed and value, it serves a range of dishes (including agedashi tofu, chicken katsu, teriyaki fish and sashimi). All meals are available in small or large sizes. There is free tea and a range of help-yourself sauces. The quality is reasonable, especially at such low prices.

Leederville

Banzai
741 Newcastle Street; tel: 08-9227 7990; Mon–Fri 11.30am–2.30pm, Tue–Sat dinner from 6pm; train: Leederville

This funky slice of Japan is always busy with students and locals who love a bargain feed. There are set meals which are good value, as well as some tempting à la carte

dishes, including fresh sashimi and mixed tempura.

Retro Betty's
127 Oxford Street; tel: 08-9444 0499; daily 11am–late; train: Leederville

This American diner-style café has a large menu of delicious burgers, all cooked to order using quality meats and fresh sourdough rolls. Order the crinkle-cut fries and a milkshake too, or their pancakes with chocolate chips.

Sayers Food
1/224 Carr Place; tel: 08-9227 0429; daily 7am–5pm, Thur until 9pm; train: Leederville

Do battle for a table at this funky café which serves tasty, fresh cuisine. There are ever-changing menus at the

Tarts Café and Home Providore

212 Lake Street; tel: 08-9328 6607; daily 7am–3pm; bus: blue CAT; map p.134 B4

Nestled amongst the terrace homes on Lake Street. For breakfast, try the scrambled eggs with feta, wilted spinach, oven-roasted tomatoes and rosemary Turkish bread. Great coffees, too.

Viet Hoa

349 William Street; tel: 08-9328 2127; daily 11am–late; bus: blue CAT; map p.134 B3

The biggest Vietnamese restaurant in Northbridge. It's a far cry from fine dining, but the food is decent and cheap.

Subiaco

Boucla

349 Rokeby Road; tel: 08-9381 2841; Mon–Sat 8am–4pm; train: Subiaco; map p.132 B2

Boucla is a treat. Fight your way past Turkish rugs to the counter, where there are no menus and no price lists. All food is cooked fresh that day,

and whatever is on display is what's left.

Café Café

Subiaco Square; tel: 08-9388 9800; daily 6.30am–5pm; train: Subiaco; map p.132 B4

Serving some of Perth's best coffee, this café is packed at weekends. They also bake great muffins and have good cooked breakfasts along with cakes, croissants and paninis.

Delizioso

94 Rokeby Road; tel: 08-9381 7796; Mon–Sat 8am–5pm, Thur until 8pm; train: Subiaco; map p.132 B3

The best thing about this little café is its Italian pizza by the slice. Toppings include eggplant and chilli, potato and rosemary, and straight cheese and herbs.

Ecco!

23 Rokeby Road; tel: 08-9388 6710; Tue–Sun 11.30am–3pm, dinner from 6pm; train: Subiaco; map p.132 B3

Sophisticated little café in the Rokeby Road shopping strip that serves fantastic pizza,

coffee, panini and a small range of mains.

Harlequin Café

1/50 Subiaco Square; tel: 08-9382 4512; Tue–Sun 8am–late; train: Subiaco; map p.132 B4

Serving casual breakfasts and lunches during the week, Harlequin steps it up a notch with its dinner and weekend breakfast service. You will find exceptional seafood and French-English influences in the dishes.

Jimmy's Noodle & Rice

Shop 4/375 Hay Street; tel: 08-9388 6337; Mon–Fri 11.30am–2.30pm, Mon–Sat dinner from 6pm; train: Subiaco; map p.132 B3

Good-value food in the heart of Subiaco. Most dishes are Indonesian, Malay, Thai or Vietnamese. The edamame beans starter can be hard to find elsewhere – if it's your first time, suck out the beans and leave the skin.

Nippon Food

479 Hay Street; tel: 08-9388 2738; Mon–Sat 11am–4pm; train: Subiaco; map p.132 B3

This postage stamp-sized eatery produces tasty teriyaki chicken to busy office crowds all week. It also has a range of inexpensive sushi. It has just three tables out front, so you might be better off taking away and heading for one of the nearby parks.

Oriel Café

483 Hay Street; tel: 08-9382 1886; daily 24 hours; train: Subiaco; map p.132 B3

The Oriel is an institution in Perth. It is the only café that is open 24 hours a day, seven days a week, and it is busy at the oddest times. The menu is extensive, and there's something for everyone.

Fremantle

Benny's Bar and Café

10–12 South Terrace; tel: 08-

Below: a server at Delizioso brandishes a tray of pizza slices.

9433 1333; daily 7am–late; train: Fremantle
Serves café-style dishes and fusion food, as well as filling Italian. Pop in for oysters, cocktails and live jazz, or settle in for some Freo people-watching on the cappuccino strip.

Cicerello's Fish and Chips
44 Mews Road, Fisherman's Wharf; tel: 08-9335 1911; daily 11am–9pm; train: Fremantle
A family favourite that has been serving fish and chips for longer than anyone can remember. Recently refurbished and extended, It has several magnificent fish tanks (the fish are decorative, not dinner) which you can watch while you queue. The kitchen closes around 8.30pm.

Flipside Burger Bar
239 Queen Victoria Street, North Fremantle; tel: 08-9433 2188; Tue–Sun 11.30am–2pm, dinner from 6pm; train: North Fremantle
Light and airy burger bar serving gourmet burgers, including some original creations such as chicken, pear and Parmesan, as well as the classic beef, egg, bacon, beetroot and cheese combo. The menu also caters to vegetarians, with chickpea patties.

Gino's
1 South Terrace; tel: 08-9336 1464; daily 6am–late; train: Fremantle
Gino's is a fixture on the Fremantle scene. You'll find families, tourists and locals all sitting down for a cappuccino while watching the world go by. The menu is big, and caters for all tastes with typical café-style fare. Always full of life.

Joe's Fish Shack
42 Mews Road, Fishing Boat Harbour; tel: 08-9336 7161; daily 11.30am–late; train: Fremantle
The decor at Joe's is nautical

Above: fish and chips, with some healthy side orders, at the Kailis Fish Market Café.

to say the least. It serves delicious light bites such as stuffed tiger prawns, crumbed Freo sardines, plus a mouth-watering seafood platter for two. There are also pasta, vegetarian and meat mains and a takeaway area outside if all you want is fish and chips to take away.

Kailis Fish Market Café
46 Mews Road, Fishing Boat Harbour; tel: 08-9335 7755; daily 7am–9pm; train: Fremantle
Kailis has been providing Perth and Fremantle with seafood for over 75 years. The fresh seafood market resides at one end of the large store and the café functions at the other, with ample seating outside on the jetty. There's basic fish and chips, plus a variety of salads, grills and desserts.

Sandrino Café
95 Market Street; tel: 08-9335 4487; daily 11am–late; train: Fremantle
A popular Fremantle eatery influenced by the flavours of the Adriatic. It prides itself on its authentic wood-fired pizza and fresh local seafood. The service is fast and friendly, with an atmosphere that oozes Fremantle.

Cottesloe, Claremont, Swanbourne and Scarborough

Barchetta
149 Marine Parade, Cottesloe; tel: 08-9385 2411; daily 6am–late; bus: 102
If you were any closer to the water, you'd be in it. Barchetta hangs over the dunes of North Cottesloe Beach, producing simple dishes with a European influence. Lunches include paella and spicy roast pumpkin salad, and the dinner menu might include chermoula lamb and crab spaghettini.

Barista
38 Napoleon Street, Cottesloe; tel: 08-9383 3545; daily 6am–10.30pm; bus: 102, 103
Serving simple yet tasty modern Australian food, Barista makes an effort to keep healthy options on the menu, and the food is always fresh.

The Blue Duck
151 Marine Parade, Cottesloe; tel: 08-9385 2499; daily 6am–late; bus: 102
Overlooking the ocean at North Cottesloe, this has been a Perth institution since it opened in 1988. Light breakfasts start at 6am, with à la carte from 7am and buffets at the weekend. From lunchtime it's always busy and you'll have to book to get a table overlooking the ocean. The menu focuses on seafood, but you'll find many other options too. If nothing else, come for coffee and eggs while enjoying the early morning light.

> People in Perth take their coffee so seriously that baristas often refuse (and can get away with it) to do anything in a café other than make coffee (no table-clearing for them), and cooking schools and cafés offer classes on how to make perfect espresso using home machines.

Children

For children, the safe, relaxed environment and relatively small-scale and open spaces make Perth perfect for adventures. With several kid-oriented attractions and events, keeping the young ones amused is simple. There are also plenty of places where both children and adults can be accommodated; beaches and parks with new play equipment, barbecues and plenty of space, often with a great view, mean that everyone can be kept happy. If you are in Perth while the school holidays are on, you'll find even more arranged activities that you can tap into by looking in the daily paper, *The West Australian*.

Activities

Extra events and projects are put on at venues during school holidays: details can be obtained from the **Perth Visitor Centre** (tel: 1300-361 351).

Adventure World
179 Progress Drive, Bibra Lake; tel: 08-9417 9666; www.adventureworld.net.au; Oct–Apr: daily 10am–5pm during school holidays, Thur–Mon out of holiday times; admission charge; train: Cockburn, then bus: 520 to Gwilliam Drive
There's unlimited use of all the rides and attractions once you have paid the quite high entry fee to enter this big adventure park. 'The Rampage' is the scariest ride of all and not for the faint-hearted. There are also giant swings, water slides, water tubing, ghost tunnels, a roller-coaster and lots more. The kids will love it – mum and dad will probably go home with a headache.

Aquarium of Western Australia (AQWA)
Hillary's Boat Harbour; tel: 08-9447 7500; www.aqwa.com.au; daily 10am–5pm; admission charge; train: Clarkson, then bus: 456
AQWA is a wonderful place for children. Western Australia has 12,000km (7,400 miles) of coastline, and five distinct coastal environments are recreated here. The highlight, however, is the walk-through aquarium representing the 'Shipwreck Coast', where sharks, loggerhead turtles, stingrays and more glide smoothly overhead within inches of the upturned faces watching them. Other highlights include a touch pool, saltwater crocodiles of the far north coast and tropical fish of the Coral Coast. The aquarium also offers the opportunity to dive and snorkel with sharks.

Awesome Festival
Various locations; tel: 08-9485 0560; www.awesomearts.com
The Awesome Festival happens every November, bringing great activities, workshops, installations and shows for children of all ages. One year, a flea circus (with real fleas) came to town, and the adults were fighting kids for a seat. Other installations have included Ixilum, a giant inflatable walk-through experience, where people are invited to wander

Below: a friendly dolphin at AQWA.

Left: the Awesome Festival features the exhibits that intrigue all ages; here, a child gets up close to the project, *Guixot De 8*, a conversion of scrap metals into interactive installations.

around on the lawns. There are barbecues, plenty of shade and a café. In another section of the park you can take a walk across the Federation Walkway, which is actually a curved glass-and-metal walk through the tree tops, looking over the Swan River. SEE ALSO PARKS, P.89–91

Maritime Museum

Victoria Quay, Fremantle; tel: 08-9431 8444; www.museum.wa. gov.au/maritime; daily 9.30am–5pm; admission charge; train: Fremantle

The spectacular building that houses the Maritime Museum was opened in 2003 and contains six themed areas: naval defence, the Indian Ocean, Fremantle and the Swan River, Hooked on Fishing, Cargoes and Tin Canoe to the America's Cup-Winning *Australia II*. *Australia II* is suspended at one end of the museum, and there are lots of quirky delights to discover. SEE ALSO MUSEUMS AND GALLERIES, P.78–9

Perth has its own free parents' newspaper. While not exactly an essay on beautiful design, it is functional and packed with info. You'll find it free at a range of locations, in particular newsagents and delis. If you are staying somewhere swish, ask reception nicely and they might be able to track one down for you. See www.kidsinperth.com.

through the various inflated 'rooms', each made from different-coloured fabric, moving and creating interesting light, shapes and more. SEE ALSO FESTIVALS AND EVENTS, P.55

Horizon – The Planetarium

Scitech, City West, Sutherland Street; tel: 08-9486 8246; Mon–Fri 9.30am–4pm, Sat–Sun and school holidays 10am–5pm; admission charge; train: City West; map p.133 E4

The Horizon Planetarium runs high-tech shows with a focus on science and space. The Planetarium is built with stadium-like seating, and the

screen wraps around the audience, creating a surreal effect.

Kings Park

Off Kings Park Road; tel: 08-9480 3634; www.bgpa.wa. gov.au; park daily 24 hours, Park Visitor Information daily 9.30am–4pm; free; bus: 102, 78, 24, 37; map p.133 D2

The Western Power Parkland (follow signs off May Drive or Fraser Avenue) is set up with children in mind. They can walk in the footprints of 'dinosaurs', play in the fort, swings and rides, or just run

If getting around the city on foot doesn't appeal to tired little ones, jump aboard the City Explorer Tram. A wooden replica tram that is allegedly similar to the ones that were common in Perth in the late 1800s will take you through historic points of the city, across the river to Burswood Resort and up to King's Park. A family pass is available for A$48, and there are 14 stops where you can hop on and off throughout the city. Barrack Street Jetty and 565 Hay Street (between Pier and Barrack) are just a couple of the stops where you can jump on. Tickets are available on board (tel: 08-9322 2006; www.perthtram.com.au/frameset/index.htm).

Perth Zoo
20 Labouchere Road, South Perth; tel: 08-9474 3551; www.perthzoo.wa.gov.au; daily 9am–5pm; admission charge; bus: 30; map p.138 A2

The Perth Zoo is great fun to explore, with 1,800 animals and 120 staff. There has been a focus over the years in creating habitats for animals that mimic their natural homes, so you will find an African Savannah area complete with red dirt and rhinos, a walk-through butterfly enclosure, and an Australian landscape where you can walk right up to a big grey kangaroo. One of the highlights is the Australian Bushwalk through recreations of different Australian ecosystems, from the arid interior to a tropical rainforest. In an Australian wetlands exhibit boardwalks wind through a huge aviary and pool complex, with a thrilling array of waterbirds and freshwater and estuarine crocodiles, including Simmo,

5m (15ft) long and weighing 600kg (1,300lb). There is a small train which can take you around the grounds, plus throughout the day you can visit various enclosures to listen to the zookeepers talk about their charges. The grounds are also lovely; you can easily spend a leisurely day here.

Scitech
City West, Sutherland Street; tel: 08-9481 5789; Mon–Fri 9.30am–4pm, Sat–Sun and school holidays 10am–5pm; admission charge; train: City West; map p.133 E4

A science discovery centre with fascinating hands-on experiments and child-oriented (sometimes icky, to an adult mind) special topics. Kids get to discover many aspects of science, including light, electricity, sound, and much more. It is all delivered in a creative, fun and very interactive way. Puppet shows are aimed at

three- to seven-year-olds, and there's a theatre performance on varying topics. Entry price includes Horizon – the Planetarium (see p.37).

Western Australian Museum
Perth Cultural Centre, James Street; tel: 08-9427 2700; www.museum.wa.gov.au/oursites/perth/perth.asp; daily 9.30am–5pm; free; train: Perth; map p.134 B3

Apart from being a genuinely interesting visit at any time of the year, the museum organises special children's activities during school holidays. There is a large hall featuring an array of stuffed animals, including a very large bison. Kids won't want to miss the dinosaurs, either. There is also a spectacular butterfly display which shows the beauty and colour of the insects. There is a dedicated area for kids, too.

Below: having fun with a street performer in Subiaco.

SEE ALSO MUSEUMS AND GALLERIES, P.77–8

Whiteman Park

Lord Street, Whiteman; tel: 08-9209 6000; www.caversham wildlife.com.au; daily 8.30am–5.30pm; free; best by car, or train: Bassendean, then bus: 337 to Lord Street and walk 350m

Only 30 minutes' drive from central Perth, this 4,050-hectare (10,000-acre) park is a great place for children. A variety of steam and diesel locomotives can take you around the park, or there's an electric tram to a picnic area. Bike hire, children's pool and mini electric cars are among the other attractions. Within Whiteman is **Caversham Wildlife Park**, worth visiting to see native animals and birds close up, and **Molly's Farm** animals. You can even have a camel ride. Caversham Wildlife Park also has a show from Tumbulgum Farm, with sheep-shearing, kelpie sheepdogs working, stockmen on horses, billy tea-making, whip-cracking, bottle-feeding baby lambs and milking a cow. The show runs several times a day for around an hour, and there is a charge.

Essentials

For essentials such as nappies, baby formula and other small child essentials, any supermarket will be able to help. The large supermarkets are **Coles** and **Woolworths**, and these are found throughout the suburbs, shopping centres and the city. There are also local supermarkets, often with longer trading hours, which can supply these items, along with basic medical needs such as headache medication, bandaids, antiseptic cream and so on.

Above: the dinos at the Western Australian Museum.

There are many late-night chemists around Perth who can also supply these things, although you will pay more for them. There will always be a pharmacist on duty who can advice on over-the-counter medication if your child is ill. Two late-night chemists are:

Beaufort Street 24 Hour Chemist
647 Beaufort Street, Mount Lawley; tel: 08-9328 7775; daily 24 hours; bus: 67, 60, 21

Stirling Drive In Pharmacy
234 Stirling Highway,

Below: cycling in Kings Park.

Claremont; tel: 08-9384 2292; daily 8am–11pm; bus: 102, 103

If you need to try to get here late at night, you are better off calling a taxi, as the wait for public transport at night can be lengthy.

If you need a doctor, either look in the Yellow Pages (there will be a yellow directory book where you are staying) or call Health Direct 24-hour advice line (toll-free: 1800-022 222). You can also find hospital information in the front pages of the White Pages (residential and business phone listings). If you need an ambulance, police or fire department, call 000 only in an emergency. Emergency hospitals include:

Princess Margaret Hospital
Roberts Road, Subiaco; tel: 08-9340 8222; www.wchs.wa.gov.au
Perth's children's hospital.

Royal Perth Hospital
Wellington Street; tel: 08-9224 2244 (emergency); www.rph.wa.gov.au

Sir Charles Gairdiner Hospital
Hospital Avenue, Nedlands; tel: 08-9346 3333; www.scgh.health.wa.gov.au
Two other city hospitals.

Environment

Australia has been in a state of drought for a number of years, and Perth hasn't been able to escape the effects. Water restrictions have been in place for a number of years: houses are only permitted to use their sprinklers two days per week, and it is recommended that they only stay on for 10 to 15 minutes. Perth is currently saving more water than the city has been targeted to, and in other environmental matters Perth is in a decent state. Energy-saving measures are encouraged, the air is clean, as are the waterways, and only on rare occasions does smog build up over the city.

Green Measures

Kings Park *(see Parks, p.89–91)* helps Perth to keep clean, with the large area of vegetation effectively cleaning much of the city's air. Perth is also one of the windiest cities on Earth, and the strong breezes that come in each day from the Indian Ocean effectively blow any pollution away from the city.

The global push for businesses and individuals to consider their carbon footprint hasn't passed Perth by, either. You'll see many cars driving around with stickers proclaiming that they are carbon-neutral (a popular site, run by **Men of the Trees**, is www.carbonneutral.com.au, a calculator that allows you to add up your entire carbon output and 'neutralise' it by paying them to plant trees) and all state government vehicles are now carbon-neutral as well. Many businesses have also taken similar steps in paying external operators to ensure that their business and employees are carbon-neutral, with some using it as a marketing opportunity.

Perth has also participated in the global movement called Earth Hour, where people are encouraged to turn off all their electricity for an hour on a Saturday night. Bigger cities in Australia have shown more public support, but the interest has been proven to be there.

There is a movement, run by the State government, called **Act Now**. The programme encourages everyone to contribute, in small or

Below: the Serpentine Dam, just outside Perth, at one of the city's main water supplies.

Left: a lookout over a dry Lake Monger after months without rain, with the city skyscrapers in the distance.

Native Flora and Fauna

The spectacular wild flowers that scatter across Western Australia's vast landscape mean spring is fondly referred to as WA's 'snow season'. Western Australia's broad climatic range sees more than 12,000 wild-flower species colour the state for about five months of the year – one of Australia's longest wild-flower seasons. Much of this, however, is not seen in the city area; you'll need to head north towards Kalbarri to see the carpets of spring everlastings and delicate orchids.

The best city place to view native flora is in Kings Park, especially during spring, where native kangaroo paws and everlastings dominate the park's scenery.

Western Australia is one of the world's most bio-diverse areas, with new species being discovered regularly, which is unheard in other parts of the world such as Europe. Meanwhile, you are most likely to see the most famous of Australia's creatures in wildlife parks, such as kangaroos and koalas, but you may be lucky and catch a glimpse if you head out to the country surrounding Perth.

everyday ways, such as by using less energy and less water, using the car less and wasting less. Part of this also includes the government committing to ensuring that 20 percent of the state's energy comes from green sources by 2010.

Recycling is popular throughout Perth homes, with each council in charge of how they run their programme. Large recycling bins are also available in some public spaces, such as beaches with food facilities. There is usually a bin for glass, for plastic, for paper and for general rubbish.

Water Restrictions

Due to the years of drought and Perth's dry climate, homeowners are changing the gardens they plant. With continuing restrictions on watering gardens, drought-tolerant plants and native plants are more popular than previously, and water-saving soil additives are popular, too.

A heavy advertising campaign has educated locals to be thoughtful of their water consumption. The dam levels are still very low (under 50 percent full), and have gone as low as 17 percent in the last five years. The WA government has been much slower to act than other states, and perhaps the continuing low dam levels are an example of this. Other major Australian cities have also introduced a ban on washing cars at home (drivers must take their cars to a car wash, which now all use recycled water), however, Perth is yet to take this measure.

A Clean City

Public littering is frowned upon in Perth. There are lots of public bins available, and locals are very proud of their clean environment. There are fines for littering, and even something as small as a cigarette butt is considered offensive, as cigarette butts are known to end up in the ocean and river, and can plug the breathing hole of dolphins. You can often see dolphins in the Swan River, which brings home the immediate threat to them.

When visiting many of Perth's beaches you'll have to walk through a dune area. There are marked paths which you should stick to, not just for safety in avoiding snakes, but also because these areas are very sensitive and often are undergoing re-vegetation. Native plants, no matter how plain they might appear, are protected in WA.

Essentials

These listings cover the sensible details that you'll need for your trip. A trip to Western Australia should be simple and relatively carefree, especially if you are aware of a few basics, such as how to keep safe and healthy (including avoiding nasty sunburns), when shops and banks open, how to make a call or post a letter and what to pack. Perthites are friendly folks and generally happy to provide assistance if you aren't sure about something or need directions. If in doubt, ask at your hotel or pay a visit to the tourist office. Note that further practical details can be found in *Children, p.39*, and *Transport, p.118–21*.

Budgeting for Your trip

Perth's economy is booming, but this generally is not reflected in visitor's costs. In general, these compare favourably with the UK and are probably on a par with the US. Public transport is very cheap (free CAT buses in Perth city centre, for example), and petrol is considerably cheaper than in the UK.

Admission charges to sights and attractions are fairly low, and often free for museums. Concession rates are available in many places on production of a valid senior or student card.

Climate

TEMPERATURES

Average temperatures are: winter: 18°C (65°F), spring: 22°C (72°F), summer: 32°C (86°F), autumn: 24°C (75°F). If these temperatures sound high, remember that WA's low humidity makes them more bearable.

WEATHER

Perth's Mediterranean-style climate means that the sun shines most days, all year.

Most of the year's rain falls during the winter months (June–Aug), easing off in spring (Sept–Nov). The city is often dry for months on end, and summer (Dec–Feb) can be very hot, with temperatures often reaching the high 30s Celsius (95–102°F).

WHAT TO PACK

Lightweight clothing is best most of the year, a few layers, plus cool, comfortable shoes or sandals. Even in winter one good sweater and scarf will be sufficient, plus an umbrella. Coats are rarely seen in Perth. Informality is the general rule, and you'll be comfortable in casual clothes just about everywhere, with the exception of better restaurants and events such as the theatre. Hats, sun-

---

Electricity is rated at 230–50 volts, 50 hertz. Standard plugs have three flat pins, and you may need an adaptor for heavier-use appliances such as hairdryers. Universal outlets for 110 volts (for shavers, etc) are found in most accommodation.

---

glasses and sunblock are strongly advised, as the sun is fierce during the summer.

Crime and Safety

EMERGENCIES

Fire, police or ambulance emergency services: dial 000. **Non-emergency police attendance:** dial 131 444.

ON THE BEACH

Parked cars are a target for petty thieves, especially those emblazoned with hire-company stickers. If possible, leave nothing in the car; your belongings are safer with you on the sand.

Beach safety extends to the ocean, too. Swim only where there are lifeguards, or the water is very placid. Take extra care on rocks where waves are pounding; occasionally, freak waves have washed people away.

SECURITY

Perth is a relatively safe place, with no unusual risks or problems, but in any big city a certain level of care must be taken. Be extra vigilant late at night, especially in

Left: public telephones are still common in Australia.

and parking, toilets and easy access routes through the city.

PUBLIC TRANSPORT
Central Area Transit (CAT) buses provide a free, frequent and wheelchair-accessible bus service.

Railway staff are available to assist wheelchair users to access metro trains. Wheel-chairs and motorised scooters can be hired from: Citiplace Community Centre, Perth Railway Station upper level; tel: 08-9325 3264; Mon–Fri 8.30am–3.45pm.
A deposit of A\$20 and proof of identification are needed; bookings are advisable. Reciprocal ACROD parking rights apply to overseas visitors for up to three months.

Embassies and Consulates
British Consular Agency
Level 26, Allendale Square, 77 St Georges Terrace;
tel: 08-9224 4700.
Canadian Consulate
267 St Georges Terrace;
tel: 08-9322 7930.
US Consulate General
16 St Georges Terrace;
tel: 08-9202 1224.

Below: one of many internet cafés in Perth.

the vicinity of bars and clubs. At this time a taxi is probably the best way to move around, unless you're just walking a short way on busier, well-lit streets. Lock car doors and don't leave valuables or bags on display in parked cars.

WILDLIFE
Be vigilant when walking in the bush, wetlands, or around lakes and rivers, near sand dunes and on Rottnest Island. Stay on paths, or where you have a clear view ahead. Snakes are the only dangerous animals you might encounter. They want to avoid you as much as you do them, and most snakes will move away when they feel the vibrations of your footfall.

Customs
Fruits and vegetables must not be brought into Australia, and any other food you're carrying must be declared. The regulations are prominently displayed on arrival, and failure to comply can result in very large penalties.

Duty free allowance is: A\$900 worth of goods (not including tobacco or alcohol, and reduced to A\$450 for under 18s); 2.25l of alcohol in total, including wine, beer and spirits; 250 cigarettes and 250g of tobacco/cigars.

Under a Tourist Refund Scheme the GST (General Sales Tax) on goods bought in Australia can be refunded on departure at the airport. Conditions are: this applies only to goods carried as hand luggage, or worn to travel; value must be a minimum of A\$300, spent in one store, shown on a single invoice; goods must be bought within 30 days of departure. To claim the tax refund, wear or carry the goods to the Tourist Refund Scheme office (beyond customs and immigration desks), together with the invoice, your passport and boarding pass.

Disabled Travellers
The starting point for disabled travellers should be the city's website: www.perth.wa.gov.au.

Access maps show how to get around and feature accessible public transport

Above: ATMs are scattered around the city.

Entry Requirements

Passports are required by all nationalities. Visas are also necessary for all but visitors from New Zealand. No vaccinations are required to visit Australia.

Health and Medical Care

If a medical problem arises while in Australia, phone the **Health Direct** 24-hour advice line: toll-free: 1800-022 2220.

BUYING MEDICINES

Pharmacies, also known as chemists, dispense prescribed medication. They also sell non-prescription medication, plus toiletries, cosmetics and film, and can often advise on minor problems.

Check **Yellow Pages** for the most conveniently located pharmacies and for listings of those that are open late.
SEE ALSO CHILDREN, P.39

DENTISTS

Many dentists practise in the city centre or nearby. Find the most convenient surgery or those with late hours listed in Yellow Pages; or call any hospital accident and emergency department.
Lifecare Forrest Chase Dental
Shop 55–57, Upper Walkway Level, 425 Wellington Street; tel: 08-9221 2777; daily 8am–8pm They take emergency cases.

MOSQUITOES

Use insect repellent, especially around still water, at dusk and in the early morning. Some mosquitoes carry viruses, so try to avoid being bitten.

INSURANCE

British citizens are covered by a reciprocal agreement with Australia which usually covers emergency health care only, not pre-existing medical conditions. Reciprocal agreements are also in place with Finland, Italy, Malta, Netherlands, New Zealand and Sweden. Passport-holders from these countries can reclaim the cost of medical treatment from Medicare in Australia. As most travellers will not qualify for free treatment, it's wise to take out health insurance. The basic cost of consulting a doctor is A$35.

SUNBURN

The Australian sun is very harsh, especially in the summer. Hats and sunglasses are essential for comfort and protection most of the year. You will burn quickly without taking any precautions. On the water, the reflection will make you burn even if you are sitting under cover. Always wear sunscreen and cover up as much as possible.

Internet

There are numerous internet cafés in Perth, especially in the Barrack Street and William Street area, and most hotels and backpacker hostels have access.
Internet Café
9 Bannister Street, Fremantle; tel: 08-9336 4900.
Internet Station
131 William Street; tel: 08-9226 5373.

Money

ATM MACHINES

These are common in the city but much less plentiful in rural areas, although you will often find an ATM in a pub or petrol station if there are no banks in town. Your ATM card will need to be part of the Plus or Cirrus network.

CREDIT CARDS

Credit cards, especially Visa, are widely accepted. Some places charge service fees.

CURRENCY

The Australian dollar (A$) is the local currency. Coin denominations are 5, 10, 20 and 50 cents, and A$1 and A$2. Notes come in denominations of A$5, A$10, A$50 and A$100.

FOREIGN EXCHANGE

Banks are generally the best places to change currency. Some hotels will exchange major currencies for guests, and there is a 24-hour agency at the airport.

TRAVELLERS' CHEQUES

International travellers' cheques will be cashed at airports, banks, hotels and motels. **Thomas Cook/**

Perth and the rest of Western Australia is eight hours in advance of GMT.

Travelex (tel: 08-9321 2896) has several city branches; the major one is in Hay Street Mall (Mon–Fri 9am–5pm, Sat 9am–1pm). Fees and rates of exchange vary between establishments. The **WA Tourist Centre** (see right) will exchange major travellers' cheques and currency. It is advisable to change your money before heading out of Perth or Fremantle, as banks are rare in the countryside.

TAXES

A General Sales Tax (GST) of 10 percent applies to most purchases. Departure tax is included in the ticket price.

Opening Hours

Retail shopping hours are generally: Mon–Thur 9am–5.30pm, Fri 9am–9pm, Sat 9am–5pm, Sun noon–5pm. Sunday opening is confined to central Perth, Fremantle and Rock-ingham. Suburban shops trade until 9pm on Thursday nights, rather than Friday nights. Banking hours are: Mon–Thur 9.30am–4pm, Fri 9.30am–5pm. Most banks are closed on Saturdays.

Postal Services

Post offices are open 9am–5pm, Mon–Fri, and the central post office in Forrest Chase also opens Saturday morning, 9am–12.30pm and Sunday, noon–4pm. See www.auspost.com.au.

Smoking

In 2006, WA banned smoking in all enclosed public places, with the exception of the Inter-national Room at **Burswood Casino**. The Healthway Quit campaign has resulted in open-air sports stadiums ban-ning smoking. If you are at a pub or venue and are in doubt as to where the designated smoking areas are, ask staff.

Telephones

MOBILE PHONES

The best course of action is to buy a 'phone card' (actu-ally simply a receipt with a PIN number that you insert in front of the number you wish to dial), which you can use with your own mobile phone (though it can also be used in public phone boxes). There are some very inexpensive deals around: simply ask the vendor for advice.

PUBLIC PHONES

Local calls from public phones cost 50¢. Long-distance calls to Australian and overseas numbers can be made from most phones, including public phones and hotels. Some public phones operate by card, available from post offices and large newsagents. For up-to-date rates and information, make a toll-free call to **Telstra** (tel: 13 22 00).

For overseas calls, dial 0011, followed by the country code and number.

Tipping

Tipping is not obligatory and not expected. That said, if you have had an especially good service and wish to tip, you will not offend. Likewise, it is not necessary to tip taxi drivers, though it is usual to round up the fare to the near-est dollar or two.

Tourist Office

Western Australia Tourist Centre

Corner of Wellington Street and Forrest Place; tel: 1300-361 351; www.wavisitorcentre.com; May–Aug: Mon–Thur 8.30am–5.30pm, Fri 8.30am–6pm, Sat 9.30am–4.30pm, Sun noon–4.30pm, Sept–Apr: Mon–Thur 8.30am–6pm, Fri 8.30am–7pm, Sat 9.30am–4.30pm, Sun noon–4.30pm; train: Perth; map p.134 A2

Located across the road from the central Perth train station, this visitor centre has a large range of touring options, and they will also book these tours for you. There is also a wide range of accommodation, transport, maps and other brochures to help with your stay.

Below: the Western Australian flag.

Excursions

Perth is an attractive city, but in order to appreciate fully the natural variety and beauty of this part of Australia, you need to venture a little further afield. In this most remote corner of Australia, locals think nothing of driving for three hours or longer to reach places that they consider close to the city. Visitors can choose to self-drive or to join an organised tour. Alternatively, bus services operate daily to many destinations (call the Transwa information line, tel: 1300-662 205, or visit www.transwa.wa.gov.au for timetables). The roads are good, the traffic is easy, and you would have to try very hard to get lost.

West of Perth

ROTTNEST ISLAND
Rottnest Island Authority; tel: 08-9432 9111; www.rottnest island.com
Rottnest Express, C Shed, Fremantle; tel: 08-9335 6406; Barrack Street, Perth; tel: 08-9421 5888
Oceanic Cruises; tel: 08-9325 1191
19km (12 miles) from Fremantle
Rotto, as the locals affectionately call Rottnest Island, is a 30-minute ferry ride from Fremantle, yet feels as though it is a world away. In its chequered history it has gone through many incarnations, including as a penal settlement and a military occupied zone, before emerging as the holiday island it is known as today. It is loved by Perthites, who escape to Rottnest for weekends of lazing on picture-postcard beaches, snorkelling in azure waters and diving among the shipwrecks that litter its coastline. Strict environmental policies keep the developers out and the traffic to a bare minimum, helping to preserve the island's sense of timelessness for future generations to enjoy.

The island is about 11km (7 miles) long and 4.5km (3 miles) at its widest. Facilities on the island are relatively basic and few and far between. Hotel accommo-

Below: a game fishing boat *(left)* and the Basin Beach *(right)* at Rottnest Island.

Left: the dramatic Pinnacles at sunset.

There are limited options for travelling by rail when making these excursions; unless you join up with a tour group (details throughout this chapter), self-driving is your best option, but remember to keep good supplies of water in your car if driving on a hot day. Details of car hire companies can be found in *Transport, p.121.*

dation is limited to the **Quokka Arms** and **Rottnest Lodge**. At peak times, accommodation is allocated by public ballot, as demand is so high. If you want to stay overnight or longer, make sure you book well in advance. Accommodation-booking is best done through the Rottnest Island Authority website *(see listing, left)*, or by visiting the office at Fremantle's C Shed markets.

Nothing sums up the pace of life on Rottnest more than the humble two-wheeler, the time-honoured form of transport on the island. With virtually no traffic on the roads, cycling is a real pleasure here, and the stunning views certainly make all the hills worth the effort. Allow about 2½ hours to make the 24km (15-mile) round trip. You can either bring your own bike (they are carried free on the ferries) or hire one from **Rottnest Bike Hire** (tel: 08-9292 5105) in Thomson Bay. Note that by law you must wear a helmet when riding a bike anywhere in WA.

If that seems like too much hard work, the Bay-seeker bus is a hop-on, hop-off service that loops between all the best beaches and the main settlement at Thomson Bay. It is designed to carry everything from surfboards to fishing rods, so it is the ideal way to get around. A day pass is very reasonable (tickets available from the Visitor Centre, *see below*). The trip from Geordie Bay to the Thomson Bay settlement is free, and a courtesy shuttle bus also plies this route.

Directly opposite the end of the jetty is the **Visitor and Information Centre** (tel: 08-9372 9732), an excellent resource for planning all aspects of your visit to Rottnest. Behind the Visitor Centre is a pedestrian shopping mall with a general store, post office, newsagent and cafés (do not be fooled by the idyllic charm of the island: chain bikes up before visiting these).

The **Basin** is generally regarded as the best swimming beach, only 10 min-utes from Thomson Bay. Other sheltered spots include **Longreach Bay**, **Little Parakeet Bay** and **Little Salmon Bay**. **Geordie Bay** boasts new holiday accommodation, shops and a picturesque bay filled with bobbing boats.

Rottnest is home to some remarkable species of coral and fish, and its crystal waters create optimum snorkelling and diving conditions. Experienced divers may want to join a trip out to one of the many wrecks lying offshore, which are havens for all kinds of sea creatures. Enquire at **Malibu Dive** (tel: 08-9292 5111), located beneath the **Dome Café** in Thomson Bay. Snorkellers can pick up an underwater trail at Parker Point – a stunning beach where the crystal-clear turquoise waters offer excellent visibility. The Visitor Centre can provide maps and pointers on the best reefs to visit.

Another nice way of exploring the island is on foot. Walking tours, run by knowledgeable volunteer guides, depart daily from the Visitor Centre. They cover a range of subjects, from Aboriginal history on the island to environ-

47

Left: at the monastery in New Norcia.

NEW NORCIA
132km (82 miles) from Perth; www.newnorcia.wa.edu.au

An easy and popular excursion from Perth (often combined with a trip to the Pinnacles) is to the Benedictine community of New Norcia, situated in the middle of the bush, a two-hour journey by car along the Great Northern Highway.

WA's only monastic town, comprising 64 buildings laid out in a cross formation, New Norcia was founded by Dom Rosendo Salvado, a missionary, in 1846. Visitors who want to explore at their own pace can take the **New Norcia Heritage Trail**, an easy 2km (11-mile) walk linking most of the major sites (details can be found at the Museum and Art Gallery, below). Alternatively, a two-hour guided walking tour departs daily from the **Museum and Art Gallery** entrance at 11am and 1.30pm (tel: 08-9654 8056). This includes entrance to the

mental issues. Most are free; some make a small charge.

SEE ALSO ABORIGINAL CULTURE, P.26–7

North of Perth

LANCELIN AND THE PINNACLES
127km (79 miles) from Perth; www.lancelin.org.au

The coastal area stretching north from Lancelin to Kalbarri is known for its perfect beaches, met by rugged gorges and wildflower plains. This area is excellent for fishing, windsurfing and snorkelling, and even facilitates activities such as sand-boarding. The coastal town of Lancelin is protected by two large rock islands and surrounded by towering sand dunes. It is reached easily from Perth by heading north along Wanneroo Road, which becomes Lancelin Road.

For a real adrenalin rush, you may want to give sand-boarding a go. **Go West Tours** (tel: 08-9791 3818) runs day tours from Perth that include sand-boarding, exploration of the Nambung

National Park and a walk through the Pinnacles.

From Lancelin, one of the most popular excursions is to the eerie **Pinnacles Desert**, in the heart of the **Nambung National Park**, about 245km (152 miles) north of Perth. Considered one of WA's most distinctive attractions, the Pinnacles Desert is an extensive area of stone monuments that rise up from the desert floor, some reaching up to 3m (15ft) high. Most major coach tours include a stop at the Pinnacles on their northbound itineraries. If you are self-driving, take Nambung National Park Pinnacles Drive off the Brand Highway. From the car park (admission charges A$10 per vehicle), it's a short walk to the Pinnacles area, although if weather conditions are poor, a 4WD might be necessary to enter the park. A circular track leads around the park, with a lookout at the northern end.

Right: the Pinnacles at sunset are popular and photogenic.

If you're heading south out of Perth along Toodyay Road, you'll reach the pretty, historic town of Toodyay after a one-hour drive, making it an attractive option for an easy day trip with a picnic lunch.

Above: Busselton Jetty.

monks' private chapel, and concludes with the opportunity to sample tasty treats from the New Norcia bakery, such as New Norcia nut cake and Dom Salvado Pan Chocolatti. These New Norcia products are super-tasty and widely available in Perth if you don't make the trek out to the community.

East of Perth

YORK
97km (60 miles) from Perth; www.yorkwa.com.au
Head east from Perth and within an hour you'll find yourself in Western Australia's lush Avon Valley, home of the historic town of York and kilometre after kilometre of farming country.

Self-driving is an excellent option if you are heading to

destinations close to the city, such as Toodyay *(see box, left)*. Another historic town is York, 35km (22 miles) south of Northam along Northam Road (from Perth, York is best accessed by taking Great Eastern Highway, then turning right onto Great Southern Highway, which leads directly into town). This tiny town is easy to explore on foot: many of the most impressive buildings are located on Avon Terrace, the main street.

South of Perth

Head south of Perth for the region's top wineries, gourmet produce (cheese, chocolate and olive oil), and dense, luscious karri and jarrah forests.

If you're catching the bus from Perth, **Transwa** has a daily service that stops at all major towns on the South Western and Bussell highways (tel: 1300 662205). **South West Coach Lines** also runs a regular service between Perth and the major southwestern towns (tel: 08-9754 1666).

BUNBURY
180km (111 miles) from Perth; www.bunbury.wa.gov.au

From Dwellingup, it's a 1½-hour drive to the southern city of Bunbury, WA's third-largest population centre. If you're self-driving, head west from Dwellingup towards Pinjarra and turn left onto South Western Highway, which leads straight to Bunbury, passing through Harvey on the way. A lush farming community, Harvey is home to the popular Harvey Fresh Juices.

One of the main attractions at Bunbury is the **Dolphin Discovery Centre** (Koombana Beach, Koombana Drive; tel: 08-9791 3088; winter: daily 9am–3pm; summer: daily 8am–4pm; admission charge). A community of bottlenose dolphins visit the beach daily to feed, and visitors can stand on the beach within an arm's reach of the mammals. Dolphin cruises depart daily during the summer, and the centre offers popular 'Swim with the Dolphins' tours.

BUSSELTON
232km (144 miles) from Perth; www.geographebay.com
The gateway to the **Margaret River Wine Region** *(see Wine Country, p.126–7),* Busselton is one of the top destinations for locals and

Above: a whale-watching point and the lighthouse at Cape Naturaliste.

visitors alike. Its location on Geographe Bay, one of only two north-facing, and therefore protected, bays in WA, also makes it perfect for families and swimmers. From Bunbury, Busselton is an easy half-hour's drive south along Bussell Highway (if you're coming from Perth, take the South Western Highway south to Busselton).

One of Busselton's most photographed features is **Busselton Jetty**. At over 1,800m (5,900ft) in length, this is the longest wooden pier in the southern hemisphere. It is packed with a range of family-friendly attractions.

The jetty's **Underwater Observatory** (tel: 08-9754 0900; Dec–Apr: 8am–5pm, May–Sept: 10am–4pm, Oct–Nov: 9am–5pm; admission charge) allows visitors to descend 8m (26ft) below sea level for amazing views of tropical and temperate fish and a range of tropical coral.

The boatshed-style **Interpretive Centre** (summer: 8am–6pm, winter: 9am–5pm; admission charge), 50m (165ft) offshore from the jetty, relates the history of the jetty. You can also watch the underwater world beneath the jetty via a marine cam, browse through the arts and crafts on display and purchase tickets for the Red Jetty Train that ferries passenger up and down the pier.

DUNSBOROUGH AND YALLINGUP
255km (158 miles) from Perth; www.australiassouthwest.com/en/Margaret+River+Wine+Region/Dunsborough/default.htm; www.westernaustralia.com
Dunsborough boasts excellent beaches, perfect for families. For more secluded beaches follow Naturalist Road, northeast of Dunsborough, to Meelup, Eagle Bay and Bunker Bay. Smith's Beach, off Caves Road and Canal Rocks Road south of Yallingup, is one of the area's best spots for surfing.

Naturaliste Road will also take you to the tip of **Cape Naturaliste** with its old lighthouse (Tue–Sun 9.30am–4pm; admission charge), built in 1903, and hiking trails. The 135km (84-mile) **Cape to**

Cape Walk leads from here to the Cape Leeuwin Lighthouse. It is not as developed as the Bibbulmun Track, but it winds through the **Leeuwin-Naturaliste National Park**, passing many natural attractions, such as Sugarloaf Rock and Three Bears, the area's best surf break. A guide to the trail is available from the Margaret River Visitor Centre. SEE ALSO PARKS, P.94

MANDURAH
74km (46 miles) from Perth
From Safety Bay, Highway 1 is the best route to Mandurah, the fastest-growing city in Australia (fast trains also link Mandurah and Perth, making the journey

Right: the stunning Kalbarri National Park.

Right: Ngilgi Cave, at Yallingup.

around an hour). Mandurah has a permanent holiday atmosphere, partly because so much of the city overlooks canals, the ocean or the Peel Inlet. Many of its restaurants, craft shops, art galleries and cultural buildings are set around Mandjar Bay, a lovely location for dining.

Inexpensive estuary and canal cruises are an excellent way to get the feel of this watery city. Several operators can be found on the jetty close to **Mandurah Art Centre**. Skippers are skilled at finding the dolphins that live in the estuary; just to see them surf and barrel-roll ahead of your cruiser is worth the fare.

Fishing is also popular, especially crabbing. On summer weekends, thousands hunt for the local blue mannas, wading the shallows with scoop nets and stout shoes, while others drop crab pots from their boats. The Mandurah crab festival, held in March, is a major annual event.

MARGARET RIVER
279km (173 miles) from Perth
From Dunsborough and Yallingup, continue south along Caves Road, turning left

at Carters Road to Margaret River. Alternatively, if you are driving from Perth, take the Busselton Bypass and head south to Margaret River on the Bussell Highway.

Margaret River is home to some of WA's top wineries, many of which also have excellent restaurants, which all in all make for very pleasant pit stops. Begin a wine tour at the **Margaret River Regional Wine Centre**, in the **Margaret River Visitor Centre** on Bussell Highway in the heart of town. It holds regular free varietal wine-tastings and can supply maps to all the wineries in the area. If you are not staying overnight, remember to designate a driver for the journey back.

SEE ALSO WINE COUNTRY, P.126–7

If you feel like continuing further afield, take the 591km (366-mile) drive up to **Kalbarri**. Other than flying, driving is the fastest way to get there, rather than taking a bus. However, **Greyhounds Australia** (www.greyhounds.com.au) and **Transwa** (www.transwa.wa. gov.au) operate direct bus services between Perth and Kalbarri. Once in Kalbarri, you can rent a vehicle from **Kalbarri Cars 4U2 Hire** (tel: 08-9937 1290) or **Kalbarri Auto Rentals** (tel: 0409-225 271). Kalbarri has long been a favourite holiday destination for West Australians, with Perthites regularly making the six-hour drive, equipped with snorkel, fishing, surfing and windsurfing gear for the outdoor opportunities on offer. However, the summer months can be scorching in Kalbarri, so for a milder experience, visit the area during winter. For an overview of Kalbarri's marine life, visit the **Kalbarri Oceanarium** (tel: 08-9937 2027; daily 10am–4pm; admission charge) opposite the marina on the foreshore. Here you'll see ocean-dwelling creatures of all shapes and sizes in a variety of large aquariums and touch pools.

Fashion

In recent years, Perth designers have been making a mark on the national scene. The WA government has employed a grant scheme similar to the one that launched New Zealand's fashion industry, and it has generated much success locally. However, West Australian style, by and large, is fairly relaxed. Suits are rarely seen outside corporate offices, and in summer just about everyone goes about in a pair of thongs (flip-flops). Major international fashion trends are usually followed but with a watered-down edge. Generally speaking, man-on-the-street fashion here is more conservative than on the east coast.

Designer

Dilettante
575 Wellington Street; tel: 08-9322 2717; Tue–Fri 10am–5.30pm, Fri until 8pm, Sat 10am–5pm, Sun noon–5pm; train: Perth; map p.134 A3
Dilettante stocks some of the world's edgier designers, including Vivienne Westwood, Luella and Rick Owens. These fashions are expensive and quirky, and definitely for those who aren't afraid to stand out (leather shirt, anyone?).

Keep an eye out for the **Perth Fashion Festival**. It usually takes place in September and is widely covered in the daily newspaper, *The West Australian*, as well as *The Sunday Times*. There are a number of free public events, showcasing local designers and models, plus many events where you can buy a ticket for entry. Many of Australia's top models come from Perth, including the internationally famous Gemma Ward, who has worked for just about every big fashion house, including Hermes, Prada, Calvin Klein, Burberry and Karl Lagerfeld.

J&T Buzza Men's Shop
836 Hay Street; tel: 08-9321 8377; Mon–Fri 10am–5.30pm, Fri until 8pm, Sat 10am–5pm, Sun noon–5pm; train: Perth; map p.134 A2
This small menswear shop is dedicated to fine clothing, including shirts, ties, cufflinks and some suiting. Father and son John and Trent Buzza work in the store, and you are guaranteed service.

Merge
G17/388 Hay Street, Subiaco; tel: 08-9380 4397; Tue–Fri 10am–5.30pm, Thur until 8pm, Sat 10am–5pm; train: Subiaco; map p.134 B1
Merge is the collaboration of several Perth designers, who banded together to find a shop space where they could sell their designs. The result is a high-end, directional store which has now been running for five years. Locals like to support their own and continue to do so.

Parker & Co.
Shop 207 Trinity Arcade, off Hay Street Mall; tel: 08-9321 8621; Mon–Fri 10am–5pm, Fri until 8pm, Sat 10am–5pm, Sun noon–5pm; train: Perth; map p.134 A2
Parker & Co. specialise in the top end of men's clothing, especially suiting. Labels include Paul Smith, Zegna, Acqua di Palma and several Italian labels.

Varga Girl
349 Murray Street; tel: 08-9321 7838; Mon–Fri 10am–5pm, Fri until 9pm, Sat 10am–5pm, Sun noon–5pm; train: Perth; map p.134 A2
The place to come for unusual designs that won't terrify you (but they might shock your credit card). Varga Girl are always keen to support local designers, and also have a good range of New Zealand fashion too. You'll find Perth's 'it' designer, Aurelio Costarella, stocked here.

Zomp
2 Bay View Terrace, Claremont; tel: 08-9384 6250; Mon–Sat 10am–6pm, Fri until 9pm, Sun noon–5pm; train: Claremont
Perth's best shoe shop, stocking international labels such as Ixus and Costume National as well as bargains such as Anna Vanilla, where a pair of leopard-print slippers will only set you back A$55. Also at: 47 King Street; tel: 08-

Left: a window display at Sportsgirl.

season stock and some current ranges.

Sportsgirl
709 Hay Street; tel: 08-9481 8282; www.sportsgirl.com.au; Mon–Fri 9am–6pm, Fri until 9pm, Sat 9am–5pm, Sun noon–5pm; train: Perth; map p.134 A2
For high-turnover, reasonably priced, trend-focused fashion, you can't beat Sportsgirl. There are finds to be had for all ages, so don't be put off by the hordes of youngsters shopping to their budget. Their accessories are great.

Target
Hay Street Mall; tel: 08-9327 3700; www.target.com.au; Mon–Fri 8am–6pm, Fri until 9pm, Sat 9–5pm, Sun noon–5.30pm; train: Perth; map p.134 A2
Target has been seen as the poor cousin to just about everything, but in the last year its collaboration with big-name designers creating capsule ranges (Stella McCartney, Josh Goot, Zac Posen) has seen people look at the store with fresh eyes. While much still can be passed over, you will find good items in there, especially in the younger women's wear.

9321 0765; Mon–Sat 9.30am–5.30pm, Fri until 9pm, Sat until 5pm, Sun noon–5pm; train: Perth City; map p.134 A2

Inexpensive

Brown Sugar
123 Rokeby Road, Subiaco; tel: 08-9380 4499; Mon–Sat 9am–5.30pm, Thur until 8pm, Sat until 5pm; train: Subiaco; map p.132 B3
The Brown Sugar chain of stores features a safe take on what you'll see in younger fashion stores. Pricing is completely reasonable, and you'll be able to pick up some good basics and more fashion-oriented pieces as well.

Country Road
307 Murray Street; tel: 08-9321 3700; www.countryroad.com.au; Mon–Fri 9.30am–5.30pm, Fri until 9pm, Sat 9am–5pm, Sun noon–5pm; train: Perth; map p.134 A2
Don't be fooled by the name: there is no 'country' style in Country Road's clothing. The ranges are moderately priced, decent quality and trend-focused without being too edgy. They are strong across women, men, children

and homewear. The city store also has a café worth visiting.

Harbour Town
840 Wellington Street; tel: 08-9321 2282; www.harbour town.com.au; Mon–Fri 9am–5.30pm, Fri until 9pm, Sat 9am–5pm, Sun noon–5pm; train: City West; bus: yellow CAT to Harbour Town; map p.133 E3
Factory-price bargains make it worth taking a trip to this outlet shopping centre. Built on the site of an old produce market, Harbour Town's dozens of stores sell discontinued lines, end-of-

Below: the Brown Sugar shop in Subiaco.

Festivals and Events

Summer weather is so reliable that you can exhaust yourself trying to get out there and see everything that is on offer. When the weather is cooler there is less on, as West Australians don't tend to react well to the cold or the very little rain that falls, and tend to stay indoors unless there is a game of AFL football to attend. Nevertheless, there are still things to see year-round. As Perth grows in profile it is attracting more and more big events, and there are more being put on by enthusiastic local bodies.

January–February

Perth Cup
New Year's Day;
www.perthcup.com
A horse-racing carnival and Perth's premier fashion event. Lots of champagne, posh frocks and outrageous hats.

Fremantle Sardine Festival
January
A celebration of the freshly caught sardine, with loads of cooked fish on offer.

Australia Day Skyworks
26 January; www.perth.wa. gov.au/skyworks/
Huge display of fireworks exploding off barges on the Swan River and the tops of the city's skyscrapers. It is the country's largest Australia Day public celebration, attracting a larger crowd than any other city's festivities.

Perth International Arts Festival
February;
www.perthfestival.com.au
Longest-established annual arts festival in the southern hemisphere, with artists from all cultural fields attending from all over the world. This festival is beginning to be con-

sidered by performers to be as relevant as big festivals such as Edinburgh. The festival covers theatre, dance, music (contemporary and classical), free public events and film.

The film component runs from December through to March and takes place at two locations. The first, the **Somerville auditorium**, is an open-air cinema at the University of Western Australia. The tradition is to bring a picnic, grab a low-slung deck-chair and enjoy the film in the open air. You are surrounded

by tall pines, which create a theatre-like effect. The second location is at **Joondalup Pines**, a similar outdoor venue. Both cinemas screen films from around the world which you won't get to see at any other cinema in Perth.

Rottnest Channel Swim
February; www.rottnestchannel swim.com.au
On a Saturday in mid-February, around 10,000 swimmers take to the water off Cottesloe Beach and swim the 20km (12.4 miles) to Rottnest Island. The departure and arrival are both worth seeing as a spectator, and the party on Rottnest afterwards is something to behold.
SEE ALSO SPORTS, P.115

March–May

Sculpture by the Sea
March; www.scultpurebythe sea.com
A free outdoor sculpture exhibition which attracts innovative art, set on and around Cottesloe Beach. Attracts around 60,000 visitors.

Left: at the Perth Cup.

Left: an exhibit at the Perth International Arts Festival.

Showcases vast WA resources, agriculture and industry, plus all the fun of the fair in Sideshow Alley.

November–December

Northbridge Festival
November; www.northbridge festival.com.au
The city of Perth and Artrage combine to bring alternative arts, theatre, dance, music, visual arts and street performance to Northbridge. It's a jam-packed weekend where you couldn't possibly get to see everything.

Awesome Children's Festival
November;
www.awesomearts.com
A 10-day family event filled with performances and installations that will entertain and enchant a range of ages.
SEE ALSO CHILDREN, P.36–7

Gay Pride March
October; www.pridewa.asn.au
Gay and lesbian parade through the streets of Northbridge.
SEE ALSO GAY AND LESBIAN, P.63

Fremantle Festival
November
Week-long celebration with street parades, parties, concerts, kites and kids' events.

Red Bull Air Race and Festival
November; www.redbullair race.com
Pilots compete against each other, demonstrating spectacular aerial manoeuvres above the Swan.

Hopman Cup
Late December to early January; www.hopmancup.com.au
An international tennis tournament which is structured as a mixed-team event; often top-10-seeded players will play for their country.

Public Holidays
New Year's Day: 1 Jan
Australia Day: 26 Jan
Labor Day: 1st Mon in Mar
Anzac Day: 25 Apr
Good Friday: Mar/Apr
Easter Monday: Mar/Apr
Foundation Day: 1st Mon in June
Queen's Birthday: 1st Mon in Oct
Christmas Day: 25 Dec
Boxing Day: 26 Dec
New Year's Eve: 31 Dec

City Food and Wine Month
March; www.perth.wa.gov.au/web/Visiting/Events/
A month-long celebration of cooking, dining and local chefs. There are tastings, demonstrations and meal deals throughout the city.

Fremantle Street Arts Festival
Easter; www.fremantle festivals.com
Entertainment with the skills and outrageous behaviour of the world's best buskers.

Drug Aware Margaret River Pro
April; www.drugawarepro.com
A world-qualifying event which attracts some of the world's best surfers to Margaret River's Main Break.

September–October

Quit Targa West
September;
www.targawest.com.au
WA's premier tarmac rally, Quit Targa West starts in Forrest Park before heading out to the hills.

Kings Park Wild Flower Festival
September and October
Shows off huge range of WA native flowers.

Spring in the Valley
mid-October;
www.swanvalley.com.au
Celebrates the people and produce of the Swan Valley with fine wines, food, art and music. Hordes of people attend – usually in groups and usually for the wine-tastings. If you like to sip in peace and quiet, perhaps you should avoid the Valley on this weekend. However if you're up for a good laugh, muck in with the locals imbibing their backyard's best.

Royal Show
early October; www.perthroyal show.com.au

Film

While Perth doesn't boast the large film production industry that Sydney does, the city's isolation and status as the capital of Western Australia, with its unique landscapes, have seen it develop a healthy industry that is well supported by the WA government through grants. The industry can and does support some producers, directors, actors and crew in a full-time capacity. Locals are also movie buffs, with a healthy range of alternatives to the main-stream multiplexes; in summer, several outdoor cinemas run for several months, taking advantage of the good weather.

Perth's Film Industry

Western Australia's rugged and varied landscape has attracted productions from around Australia. Big-name Australian director Philip Noyce, whose better-known films include *Clear and Present Danger*, *The Saint*, *The Bone Collector*, *Patriot Games*, *Dead Calm* and *Newsfront*, shot in WA in 2002 when filming *Rabbit-Proof Fence*, which tells the story of three Aboriginal children who, when taken from their parents as part of the 'Stolen Generation' *(see Aboriginal Culture, p.26)*, flee and walk the 1,500km (932-mile) rabbit-proof fence home. Based on a true story, the rabbit-proof fence was installed in the 1930s with the hope that it would keep the devastating rabbit population from encroaching across the country.

In 2006, a psychological drama called *Last Train to Freo* was shot entirely on a Transperth train. The film tells the story of two thugs who are on the train when a young woman boards, and the ensuing tension between the three and other passengers. It was directed by actor Jeremy Sims.

Other films such as *Japanese Story*, starring Toni Collette, were produced in Western Australia, and in 2008 Baz Luhrmann's (*Moulin Rouge*, *Romeo + Juliet*, *Strictly Ballroom*) epic *Australia*, starring Nicole Kidman and Hugh Jackman, was filmed in the north of the state.

One of Perth's most famous exports was actor Heath Ledger. Ledger, who passed away in 2008, grew up in Perth attending the prestigious Guildford Grammar. Ledger was first noticed on the Australian film scene in 1997 with *Blackrock* and *Two Hands*. After breaking into Hollywood with *A Knight's Tale* and *10 Things I Hate about You*, Ledger featured in some underwhelming roles, before Ang Lee's *Brokeback Mountain* saw him commended with an Oscar nom-

Below: actor Heath Ledger (1979–2008).

ScreenWest, the state's film funding body, receives over A$4 million each year from Lotterywest. Lotterywest is responsible for running the cash lotteries in WA, but unlike other states in Australia, Lotterywest is not-for-profit, and redistributes around A$145 million each year back into the community through a wide variety of grants. Screen-West plans to focus on drama productions, indigenous productions, documentaries and digital production in their funding up until 2011.

In 2008 a Perth-made film called *Two Fists, One Heart* was completed. However, this was no mean feat. The government's funding body, ScreenWest, pulled its initial support when the Arts Minister, Sheila McHale, realised that the man behind the project was a controversial figure, boxer and alleged-dodgy-bloke Rai Fazio. Rai subsequently sought help from private backers, raising A$3 million for the film. The producer behind the locally produced *Rabbit-Proof Fence* also came on board and found the money needed to get the project going.

ination. His tragic and sudden death at the age of 28 saw the world's paparazzi descending on Cottesloe Beach for his funeral. Ledger's family still lives in Perth.

Cinemas

Many cinemas in Perth offer a cheap-ticket day each week, usually Tuesday but sometimes Wednesday; check with each cinema.

The Astor

659 Beaufort Street, Mount Lawley; tel: 08-9370 1777; www.astorcinema.com.au; daily from 10am; bus: 67, 21

Heritage-listed Art Deco building showing modern and classic films.

Camelot Outdoor Cinema

16 Lochee Street, Mosman Park; tel: 08-9385 4793; www.luna palace.com.au; daily from 10am; bus: 103

Charming Art Deco building with theatre space. Cinema is in a garden, with deckchairs, a bar and food available. You may BYO food, but not alcohol.

Cinema Paradiso

164 James Street, Northbridge; tel: 08-9227 1771; www.luna palace.com.au; daily from 10am; train: Perth; bus: blue CAT; map p.134 A3

Shows a mix of art-house films, often subtitled.

Luna Cinema

155 Oxford Street, Leederville; tel: 08-9444 4054; www.luna palace.com.au; daily from 10am; train: Leederville

Luna has one large cinema, many small studios and an outdoor one for summer, where there's a bar and you can bring a picnic. Luna also runs several festivals throughout the year, including a Manga (Japanese animation) one and a Bollywood one. Each Monday night a different 'double' is screened, starting at 7.30pm. If you can stay up late on a Monday night, it's great value.

Somerville Auditorium

University of WA, Nedlands; tel: 08-9488 1732; www.perth festival.com/lotterywestfestival films; Dec–Mar: approximately 8.30pm; bus: 102, 103; map p.136 A2

This is the main venue for Perth Festival films; there's

another at the Joondalup campus of Edith Cowan University. Somerville is very atmospheric, with deckchairs, and lined with tall pine trees; Joondalup is beside an illuminated lake.

The Windsor

98 Stirling Highway, Nedlands; tel: 08-9386 3554; www.luna palace.com.au; daily from 10am; bus: 102, 103

A two-cinema Art Deco building which has the lovely feel of the grand age of cinema.

Below: the Luna Cinema.

Food and Drink

Stereotypically, Perth is thought of as the country cousin to Australia's cosmopolitan centres of Sydney and Melbourne. However, thanks to successive waves of immigration from all over the world, an abundance of fresh produce and the wealth from a sustained resources boom, Perth's food has come into its own in recent years, while the riches of the Margaret River vineyards also add splendid wines to this mix. A new wave of dynamic chefs enthused about local produce means that you'll find a brand of modern Australian cuisine in Perth that easily ranks alongside that found elsewhere in the country.

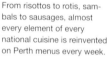

Origins and Influences

Although Western Australia's first settlers went to the trouble of establishing the state's first vineyards in the Swan Valley, Western Australian cuisine remained defiantly British until well into the 1950s. The first inklings of a Mediterranean influence developed in the 1920s when many Italian and Slavic immigrants arrived, and flourished in the post-war immigration boom. However, it is only since Asian immigration, the advent of fusion cuisine and the food revolution of the 1980s that Australia developed the dynamic

cuisine that defines the country today.

Such is the profusion of flavours in contemporary Perth that you would have to scour myriad menus to find anything akin to the traditional British old-style cuisine of yesteryear. These days a roast of prime Western Australian lamb is more than likely to have a Moroccan, Mediterranean or Indian mien, and fish dishes will, in all probability, be accented with Thai or Vietnamese flavours. Even the good old Aussie pavlova has taken a back seat to desserts such as black sticky rice pudding

or coconut fried ice cream. From risottos to rotis, sambals to sausages, almost every element of every national cuisine is reinvented on Perth menus every week.

Perth Cuisine

POPULAR DISHES

Chilli mussels, made with locally farmed mussels, would have to rate as an all-time Perth favourite, while chargrilled marron, served with a lime beurre blanc, as it is by **Lamont's** *(see p.103)*, the East Perth restaurant that first introduced these indigenous freshwater crustaceans to the national table,

Below: fresh fruit on offer at the Station Street Markets in Subiaco.

Left: a beautifully prepared lobster dish at Fraser's Restaurant *(see p.100–101)*.

Boutique olive oil production is at an all-time high, with almost every region in the state offering a unique blend of extra virgin olive oil.

Locally grown persimmons, tamarillos and tropical fruits have joined a long list of staples, such as stone fruits, apples, pears and myriad Asian vegetables, that are sought after at home and in Southeast Asia. New Norcia panforte and biscotti are exported all over the world. Locally made chocolates and preserves can also compete against overseas imports, and there is an array of artisan yoghurts on offer. But as an example of the much-vaunted West Australian audacity, the local black truffles that are now appearing on Perth tables would have to win hands down.

Eating In

If there's anything Perthites enjoy more than dining out, it is eating in, and being invited to someone's home is the best compliment you can receive. Home cooking has also undergone a revolution in Perth in recent years, where dishes such as beef rendang, green curry and couscous have taken their place alongside roasts, stews and grills. Long, hot summers ensure that the barbecue is a local institution, while picnics are an essential component of an outing to an outdoor cinema (see Film, p.57).

If someone invites you to bring a chop for the barbie, you can be assured they mean a dozen or more well-marinated chops. Understatement is as Australian as BYO (bring your own wine/

Northbridge is the place to come to find many of the world's cuisines in one district: during the day you can pop between Italian, Indian, Chinese, Vietnamese and European bakers, butchers and provedores. At night these places close and are taken over by restaurants serving meals in these cuisines.

is considered a rare treat. Another local favourite are **The Witch's Cauldron**'s garlic prawns *(see p.106)*, which have been served unchanged at this Subiaco restaurant for 30 years. Locals can't seem to get enough, either, of slow-braised lamb shanks encased in pastry, as prepared at **Darlington Estate Winery Restaurant** in Darlington *(see p.107)*.

LOCAL PRODUCE AND ARTISAN FOODS

A key feature of the local cuisine is its excellent produce. Long renowned for its high-quality lamb, beef and wheat, as well as for its fish, fruit and vegetables, the state has seen a massive increase in the production of gourmet produce in recent years. Boutique bakeries, artisan and organic butchers and speciality cheesemakers thrive thanks to an upsurge of public interest in food, not to mention a 30-year-long resources boom that has seen sustained growth levels significantly higher than the national average. Little wonder, then, that locally produced Wagyu beef at A$120 per kilogramme is finding its way onto Perth's most discerning tables, or that Kervella artisan goat's cheese is now a staple on many a restaurant and café menu. The superbly succulent and tender White Rocks veal is beloved of the finest east-coast eateries. Farmed barramundi and trout have now joined marron, rock lobster, Patagonian toothfish, sardines, dhufish and snow crab at the table. Shellfish is varied and abundant, and even Japanese chefs are demanding Margaret River venison.

Above: picnicking in the Swan Valley on a nice day.

beer), and local custom decrees you never turn up for a meal at someone's house without a bottle of good wine.

Where to Buy Food

Boatshed Fresh Food
40 Jarrad Street, Cottesloe; tel: 08-9284 5176; daily 6am–late; train: Cottesloe, bus: 102, 103
The Boatshed is a foodie's mecca. Inside you'll find a fishmonger, butcher, bakehouse and deli. All offer top-quality products; the cheese counter in particular always has a fantastic selection. Samples are available throughout the store, and the ready-made meals are very good, as is the quality and range of the fresh produce. There is also a florist and a large range of gourmet groceries.

Chez Jean-Claude Patisserie
333 Rokeby Road, Subiaco; tel: 08-9381 7968; Mon–Fri 6am–6pm; train: Subiaco; map p.132 B2
This is a little slice of baking heaven on the far end of Rokeby Road. It does a roaring trade in rolls, sandwiches, pies, sweet treats and cakes produced by French-Swiss

baker Jean-Claude. There's no seating, but it's so good you won't mind taking away.

Claremont Fresh
333 Stirling Highway, Claremont; tel: 08-9383 3066; daily 7am–7pm; train: Claremont, bus: 102, 103
This popular shop sells top-quality fresh produce plus an excellent range of gourmet products, including a great selection of cheese and some ready-made meals. There is a butcher in the shop: if you are in a rush they will even cook and prepare your meat for you.

David Jones Foodhall
622 Hay Street Mall; tel: 08-9210 4000; Mon–Fri 9.30am–6pm, Thur until 7pm, Fri until 9pm, Sat 9am–5pm, Sun noon–6pm; train: Perth; map p.134 A2
Located on the ground floor of Perth's swishest department store, the David Jones Foodhall is a mecca for any foodie. Aside from the produce available for purchase, there is an oyster bar serving fresh and cooked oysters with champagne, a sushi bar, a noodle and curry bar (serving a top-notch pad thai), fresh sandwiches, a coffee and chocolate bar and a fresh

juice bar. Take some time out from shopping to relax with some top-quality food.
SEE ALSO SHOPPING, P.108–9

The Earth Market
14/375 Hay Street, Subiaco; tel: 08-9382 2266; Mon–Sat 9am–5pm; train: Subiaco; map p.132 B3
This shop-cum-café specialises in whole and organic foods. Come here to buy organic veg and a large range of healthy options.

Fremantle Markets
Cnr South Terrace and Henderson Street; Fri 9am–9pm, Sat 9am–5pm, Sun 10am–5pm, Mon 10am–5pm; train: Fremantle
Complete with fruit and vegetables, seafood, freshly baked bread, cheeses, coffees, herbs and spices and gourmet foods.
SEE ALSO SHOPPING, P.109

Kailis Bros Fish Market
101 Oxford Street, Leederville; tel: 08-9443 6300; Mon–Sat 7am–6pm, Sun 7am–5pm; train: Leederville
Kailis is just about the biggest seafood supplier in WA. Their public fish market is beautiful; choose from a wide range of whole fish, mussels, oysters, crabs, lobster, scallops and other seasonal delights on ice

beds, plus filleted fish, marinated and pre-made mixes. They also stock a small range of cookbooks, knives, bread and smallgoods.
SEE ALSO CAFÉS, P.35; RESTAURANTS, P.102

Kakulas Bros
183 William Street, Northbridge; tel: 08-9328 5285; Mon–Sat 8am–6pm; train: Perth; map p.134 A3

A stalwart on the Perth food scene, come here for bargain prices on bulk produce. They stock a huge range of Continental ingredients.

Mondo's Butchers
824 Beaufort Street, Inglewood; tel: 08-9371 6350; Tue–Fri 8am–6pm, Sat 7am–2pm; bus: 67, 21

Vince Garreffa is a local legend. He has recently revamped his Mondo's Butchers, expanding his extensive range of meat to include ready-to-cook meals such as gourmet pies and quiches (all made on site without preservatives and with top-quality meat), vacuum-sealed meats such as emu, kangaroo and crocodile, bread and home essentials. Vince is the man behind White Rocks veal,

which is favoured by the country's top chefs.

The Re Store
73 Lake Street, Leederville; tel: 08-9328 1032; Mon–Sat 8am–6pm, Sat 8am–5pm; train: Perth; map p.134 A3

The Re Store is a joy, selling Italian meats, cheeses, sweets, bread and more. The Leederville branch has a liquor store with a very good range and good prices, and also a counter where you can have fresh rolls filled with a range of fillings. Also at: 231 Oxford Street, Leederville; tel: 08-9444 9644; train: Leederville

Station Street Markets
41 Station Street, Subiaco; tel: 08-9382 2832; Fri, Sun 9am–5.30pm; train: Subiaco; map p.132 B4

A large, cheap range of fresh fruit and veg. There are also shops selling bulk groceries such as nuts, cereals, rice and so on, as well as an excellent French baker.
SEE ALSO SHOPPING, P.109

Torre Butchers
41–43 Lake Street, Northbridge; tel: 08-9328 8317; Mon–Sat 7am–5pm; train: Perth; bus: blue CAT; map p.134 A3

Torre is known as one of the

People in Perth tend to eat dinner around 7pm, but with the introduction of daylight saving during summer this can go as late as 9pm.

best butchers in town. They have a wide selection of hard-to-find meats and can offer expert advice as well as prep them for you.

Tran's Emporium
358 Newcastle Street, Northbridge; tel: 08-9228 3099; daily 8am–6pm; bus: blue CAT; map p.134 A4

As the name suggests, you'll find a large range at Tran's. It is a specialist Asian supplier, so come here for unusual pastes, sauces and hard-to-find veg. There are also Asian cooking implements, crockery and other interesting items.

La Vigna
302 Walcott Street, Mount Lawley; tel: 08-9271 1179; www.lavigna.com.au; Mon–Sat 10am–8pm; bus: 67, 21

Mike Tamburri has one of the finest wine collections around, so if you want good advice and a great range, this is the place.

Below: fresh fish on offer at Kailis Bros Fish Market.

Gay and Lesbian

Perth's gay scene is minor compared to a city such as Sydney, where gay couples can interact in exactly the same way that straight couples can. But Perth, in many respects, remains a conservative community, and while homophobia is mostly a thing of the past, gay couples do not enjoy the same sense of confidence that is found in other big cities. Having said that, the gay community is alive and well, with a few select popular hangouts. The favoured and most tolerant hangouts for gay and lesbian locals and visitors are mostly in the inner city, such as Northbridge, Highgate and Mount Lawley.

Accommodation

These hotels are the most gay-friendly or in the case of Pension of Perth, gay-owned and operated.

Chifley on the Terrace
185 St Georges Terrace; tel: 08-9226 3355; www.chifley hotels.com; $$–$$$; train: Perth; map p.134 A2
The Chifley is a small hotel located, unsurprisingly, right on the terrace, in this case, St George's Terrace. The rooms aren't huge but are pleasant, and downstairs you'll find a great bar and restaurant.

Hotel Northbridge
210 Lake Street, Northbridge; tel: 08-9328 5254; www.hotel northbridge.com.au; $$; bus: red or blue CAT; map p.134 B4
This beautiful old building was recently restored and now sports lovely rooms kept in style with the era of the building. Downstairs is a popular restaurant and bar, and the hotel is only a short stroll to Hyde Park in the north and Perth city to the south. It is out of the noise of Northbridge and is situated on a tree-lined, mainly residential street.

Pension of Perth
3 Throssell Street; tel: 08-9228 9049; www.pensionperth. com.au; $$; bus: red or blue CAT
Run by a gay couple, this bed and breakfast offers comfortable, cosy accommodation and a relaxed atmosphere for those seeking something more personal than a big hotel.
SEE ALSO HOTELS, P.70

Venues

Connections Nightclub
96 James Street, Northbridge; tel: 08-9328 1870; www.connectionsnightclub.com; Fri 8pm–late, Wed, Sat 10pm–late; map p.134 A3
Connections (or 'Connies' as it's affectionately known), is Australia's longest-running gay and lesbian nightclub, with more than 30 years of fabulous tunes and high heels behind it. Renovated for its 30th birthday, Connies is now resplendent in marble and mirrors, and has a small rooftop garden with city skyline views.

The Court Hotel
50 Beaufort Street; tel: 08-9328 5292; Sun–Wed noon–midnight, Thur–Sat noon–2am; bus: blue CAT to Aberdeen Street Art Centre; map p.134 B3
The Court Hotel has recently had several million spent on a revamp, and now boasts an

Left: hitting the streets for the annual Pride Parade.

ionistas turn out in droves to celebrate fashion and to raise money for the WA Aids council. Tickets to the evening cost around the A$200 mark, and for that punters get a fashion parade, pre-dinner drinks, a top-quality dinner, all alcohol, entertainment and a goodie bag. Guests can also bid on donated items such as diamond jewellery and holidays.

Safety

Perth is a reasonably safe place to live and visit, with very few homophobic incidents, but it is always wise to stay alert to the possibility of running into predjudices, especially once out of the city. Generally speaking, attitudes in the countryside are more conservative. In Perth, many locals may not be as used to seeing open displays of affection between gay and lesbian couples as in some other cities, but by the same token, the population is generally well educated and tolerant. In the main, being openly gay rarely causes problems. However, at night in some districts where heavy drinking occurs at weekends (Northbridge, for example), it is worth steering clear of large groups of drunk men.

impressive bar, along with its outdoor pizzeria and other areas. At weekends the place heaves until the small hours and often a fabulous drag show is the highlight of the night. There is also a restaurant which has received good reviews. Straight-friendly, too.

Perth Steamworks
369 William Street, Northbridge; tel: 08-9328 2930; www.perth steamworks.com.au; daily noon–late; bus: blue CAT to William Street; map p.134 B4
This steamworks has a six-

man pool, dry sauna and steam room. It's a popular hangout in which to relax, or for meeting men who might be interested in slightly more. There are fetish rooms, private cubicles and plenty of condoms and information regarding safe sex.

Festivals
Pride
www.pridewa.asn.au
Each year, October's Pride Festival marks a big week in the gay and lesbian calendar, (with the exception of 2007, when amid talk of unpaid debts, no festival was held). The Pride Parade, held on a Saturday night, is not nearly as big as Sydney's Mardi Gras, but is still a night for celebration and attracts as much of a straight crowd as it does a gay and lesbian crowd. Visit the website to check for updates.
Styleaid
www.styleaid.com.au
This gala event happens each year towards the end of August. The city's fash-

Left: the gay-friendly Pension of Perth bed and breakfast.

History and Architecture

50,000 BC
Aborigines populate all of Australia.

1606
First authenticated voyage to Australia, by the Dutch ship the *Duyfken* ('Little Dove').

1616
Dutch explorer Dirk Hartog in the Eendracht makes first authenticated landing in Western Australia, at Shark Bay.

1696–7
Discovery of Swan River by Willem de Vlamingh.

1826
King George Sound is occupied by convicts from Sydney under Major Lockyer.

1828
British government approves founding of Swan River Colony; appoints Captain Stirling lieutenant-governor.

1829
Formal possession of the colony is taken by Captain Fremantle; in June Stirling arrives to found the colony. Pitched, corrugated-iron roofs are the norm in residential housing and as architecture is dictated by climate, verandas are popular as they keep the houses cooler.

1831
Stirling made governor. King George Sound convict settlement is withdrawn. First newspaper issued.

1843
Petitions for the introduction of convicts.

1850
Convicts sent from Britain to meet labour shortage and help build Perth.

1856
Queen Victoria grants Perth city status. Gothic Revival-style architecture dominates churches and cathedrals.

1868
Convict transportation ends.

1870
Colony gains representative government.

1871
Municipalities Act and Elementary Education Act passed; first private railway built.

1877
Telegraph links Perth and London via Adelaide.

1881
Eastern railway links Perth, Fremantle and Guildford.

1886
Kimberley goldfield proclaimed, the first of several in Western Australia.

1890
WA gains responsible government. Sir John Forrest forms first government.

1892
Construction of Fremantle Harbour begins.

1893
Paddy Hannan's Kalgoorlie find becomes 'The Golden Mile', and the gold rush transforms Perth.

1899
Women get the vote, ahead of Britain, Canada and the US. Perth Electric Tramway begins to supersede horse transport. The Boer War breaks out and 1,231 WA men go to South Africa; 126 die, one wins the Victoria Cross. Back in Perth, the building of the Goldfields Water Supply commences (completed January 1903). Towns are seeing the pay-off from the gold rush, with their public buildings becoming grander and more embellished. Today these buildings are usually pubs.

1901
Commonwealth of Australia inaugurated 1 January. WA becomes a state of federal Australia.

1901
WA joins the British Empire. Duke of York visits Perth and names Kings Park.

1904
His Majesty's Theatre is built, enjoying the stylistic excess of the period.

1911
University of Western Australia opens. Homes are 'federation' style; there are still many examples of this in areas such as Mount Lawley.

1914–18
6,000 Western Australians die and thousands more are wounded in World War I.

1917
Trans-Australian Railway links WA to eastern states.

1920S
Fremantle is busiest oil-fuelling port in Australia; world's first long-distance air service operates from Perth centre.

1929
Amid centenary celebrations of the 1829 founding, George V declares Perth a 'Lord Mayoralty', and Fremantle becomes a city.

1931
The Great Depression results in one in four Perth men being jobless; a 5,000-strong protest march ends in violence and arrests.

1930s
Depression-fighting project creates Langley Park and Riverside Drive by river reclamation.

1933
State of WA votes to opt out of federation, but the UK government rules the move 'unconstitutional'.

1938
The Regal Theatre in Subiaco is built and remains a good example of the popular Art Deco buildings of the time.

1939–45
Perth men and women serve in World War II; city prepares for air raids. Fremantle is essential to the war effort, as the secret base for 170 Allied submarines. Sunderland and Catalina flying boats are based on the Swan. Victory in the Pacific on 15 August 1945 (VP Day).

1954–8
More of the Swan River reclaimed for building of the Narrows Bridge and Freeway.

1959
First television service begins.

1962
Perth hosts Empire Games.

1968
Worst tremors in memory rock Perth as Meckering, 130km (80 miles) east of the city, is destroyed by an earthquake.

1971
Concert Hall opens, deemed as important an icon as the Town Hall (1870).

1978
HMAS *Stirling* is naval base for Australia's submarine fleet.

1979
WA celebrates first 150 years.

1983
Australia II wins America's Cup off Rhode Island. It is the first non-American entrant to win.

1987
America's Cup held in Fremantle, putting the port city on the world map.

1999
World's earliest known life form, 3.5 billion-year-old stromatolites, found in outback and brought to Perth's WA Museum.

2001
Labor regains state power after eight years in opposition.

2004
Perth Convention Centre opens.

2008
Plans are unveiled for a new city waterfront development.

Hotels

Perth is a small city where you can stay in the very centre at moderate cost and walk easily to theatres, entertainments, the park and the river. However, easy travel on fast trains, clean, air-conditioned buses, smooth roads and relatively inexpensive taxis means you can stay at the beaches or in leafy suburbs if you prefer, and still quickly get into the centre of Perth and Fremantle. The city has a wide range of hotel options, from small boutique hotels through to international five-star chains, but there is often a shortage of rooms available, so be sure to book in advance of arrival.

Accomodation in Perth

If you crave full-service, luxury hotel accommodation there's little choice but the hotels on Adelaide Terrace, the city riverside and at Burswood. However, high-quality, clean accommodation tends to be available in all price ranges, at moderately priced hotels, bed-and-breakfast houses, and even backpackers' hostels all across the metropolitan area.

Great value and lavish comfort can also be experienced at some bed-and-breakfast establishments. Generally speaking, the B&B accommodation tends to match the area. Alternatively, you could stay in a rural location in the Swan Valley or the Darling Ranges, which are still only 30 minutes from the city. Staying outside

Perth, even for a short time, is a fast way to get the feel of 'real Australia'.

Swan River and Kings Park

The Richardson Hotel Suites and Spa

32 Richardson Street; tel: 08-9217 8888; www.the richardson.com.au; $$$$; bus: red CAT; map p.133 D3

The Richardson is Perth's newest boutique hotel. Boasting a fine-dining restaurant, Opus, and one of Perth's best day spas, the hotel has a range of rooms available, plus pool and sauna. The Richardson has counted pop stars such as Pink and Christina Aguilera as guests, so they must be doing something right.
SEE ALSO PAMPERING, P.87

Riverview on Mount Street

42 Mount Street; tel: 08-9321 8963; www.riverviewperth.com.au; $$–$$$; bus: 103, 37; map p.133 E2

These serviced apartments are in a great location. Mount Street runs down one edge of Kings Park, and at the bottom (it is an incredibly steep

street) there is a pedestrian flyover that crosses the freeway, quickly depositing you at the top of St Georges Terrace near the Mill Street intersection. At the bottom of the building is the very cool Bouchard café, which serves excellent fare.

City Centre

Aarons All Suites Hotel

12 Victoria Avenue; tel: 08-9318 4444, toll-free: 1800-000 675; www.aaronssuites.com.au; $$; bus: red CAT; map p.134 B1

A range of modern, fully equipped apartments, with a rooftop spa and a barbecue

Below: the Duxton hotel.

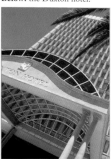

Left: great views and stylishly retro design at Rydges.

If you have left it late to book accommodation, a good website to try is **www.wotif.com.au**. Hotels advertise special room rates, and there are some bargains to be had. You can book here usually a couple of weeks in advance, but the closer to the day you are looking for, the better bargain you'll find. The only catch is you will have restricted choice, and hotel rooms in Perth, especially over weekends, can be hard to find.

area. Very near the CBD and Adelaide Terrace and within walking distance of the river and shops.

Aarons Hotel
70 Pier Street; tel: 08-9325 2133, toll-free: 1800-998 133; www.aaronsperth.com.au; $$; bus: red CAT; map p.134 B2

Centrally placed, on a free CAT bus route around Perth, this hotel is modern and comfortable, with a bright bar and grill and very good, friendly service.

Bailey's Parkside Hotel-Motel
150 Bennett Street; tel: 08-9325 3788; toll-free: 1800-199 477; www.baileysmotel.com.au; $; bus: red or blue CAT; map p.135 C2

Homely hotel opposite park, within walking distance of the city centre. Comfortable units are complemented by an on-site swimming pool and barbecue. Restaurant serves 'home-style' cooking, and the room tariff includes a Continental breakfast.

Criterion Hotel Perth
560 Hay Street; tel: 08-9325 5155, toll-free: 1800-245 155; www.criterion-hotel-

perth.com.au; $$; bus: red CAT; map p.134 B2

In a central location opposite the historic Perth Town Hall and housed in a beautifully restored Art Deco building in the main shopping area, with a 'British pub' in the basement.

Duxton
1 St Georges Terrace; tel: 08-9261 8000, toll-free: 1800-681 118; www.duxton.com; $$$$; bus: blue CAT; map p.134 B1

Beautifully renovated hotel in a heritage building (not that you would actually know by looking at it), formerly Perth's

old tax office. Close to the Perth Concert Hall, Swan River and shops, the Duxton is known for its lavish breakfast buffet.

Hyatt Regency Perth
99 Adelaide Terrace; tel: 08-9225 1234; www.perth.regency.hyatt.com; $$$$; bus: red CAT; map p.135 C1

Pool, tennis court, fitness centre, sauna and everything rightly expected of a 5-star hotel. You can do elegant dining or café-style, or prop up one of several bars. The food options here are very good, from the Singapore-colonial style of Joe's Oriental Diner to the revamped Café and the

Below: the Art Deco exterior of the Criterion Hotel.

Above: the quirky facade and sign welcome you to the Miss Maud Swedish Hotel.

sublime Gershwin's fine dining. They serve a lovely high tea in the atrium-style seating area at weekends. Touring musicians often stay here. Close to river, shopping, CBD and entertainments.

The Melbourne
Cnr Hay and Milligan streets; tel: 08-9320 3333; www.melbourne hotel.com.au; $$–$$$; train: Perth; map p.133 E2
The Melbourne is located in the heart of the CBD, and offers an alternative to the polished new hotels of the city. With 34 rooms restored to reflect the hotel's gold rush-era period character, it also offers a public bar downstairs and dining in either M Cafe or the Melbourne Restaurant. The bar is popular on Friday night with the city's after-work crowd, so you can feel in the midst of it easily.

Miss Maud Swedish Hotel and Restaurant
97 Murray Street; tel: 08-9325 3900, toll-free: 1800-998 022; www.missmaud.com.au; $$; bus: red CAT; map p.134 B2

Price categories are for a standard double room per night without breakfast.
$$$$ = A$250 plus
$$$ = A$175–$250
$$ = A$100–$175
$ = under A$100

With a quaint and quirky auberge-styled exterior, this hotel is close to the inner city and shops. True to its name, it offers the dining option of a smorgasbord in the alfresco dining area, where there is a popular coffee shop. Miss Maud is actually a real person, running a popular café and patisserie chain with outlets across Perth. Rooms are suitably Scandinavian, with a dash of Alpine style.

New Esplanade Hotel
18 The Esplanade; tel: 08-9325 2000; www.newesplanade. com.au; $$; bus: blue CAT; map p.134 A2
Close to the river and Barrack Street Jetty and within easy reach of city shopping. No restaurant, but breakfast is served in the Esplanade Café. Some suites have a full kitchen.

Rydges
815 Hay Street; tel: 08-9263 1800, reservations: 1300-857 922; www.rydges.com; $$$; train: Perth; map p.134 A2
The Rydges hotel is conveniently located on the corner of Hay and King streets in the CBD and is a reasonably large hotel for such CBD convenience. The large rooms have recently been renovated in a modern-retro and tactile style; ask for a room on a high-numbered floor for spec-

tacular views from the big windows. Downstairs is the very popular CBD Bar and Restaurant, which packs out on Friday nights.

Sheraton Perth
207 Adelaide Terrace; tel: 08-9224 7777; www.sheraton.com/ perth; $$$$; bus: 103, 158; map p.134 C1
Close to the CBD, main shopping areas, Cultural Centre and entertainments, with the pampering luxuries of a heated pool, gym and steam room. All rooms have views of Swan River, and the hotel has had a recent refurbishment. It is also the only one in Perth to employ an old-school butler. Brook has worked at the Sherton for more years than he will reveal and looks after guests in the Presidential Suite. He has served the world's famous folk, including Elton John, Elle MacPherson, Olivia Newton-John and countless others. The Sheraton's fine-dining restaurant, Origins, is also worth a visit.

Sullivans Hotel
166 Mounts Bay Road; tel: 08-9321 8022, toll-free: 1800-999 294; www.sullivans.com.au; $$; bus: blue CAT; map p.133 E1
Small family-owned hotel on the river below King's Park escarpment that offers free internet access.

East Perth

Holiday Inn Burswood
Great Eastern Highway,
Burswood; tel: 08-9362 7777,
toll-free: 1800-001 650;
www.burswood.holiday.inn.com;
$$$; bus: 24, 296
Perth's first new, purpose-
built hotel for 12 years
opened in 2005, and is a
less expensive option on the
same riverside site as the
Intercontinental Burswood
Resort *(see below)*. Holiday
Inn patrons have access to
all Intercontinental restau-
rants and facilities, plus
have their own restaurant-
cum-bar, Sirocco, serving
modern Australian food.

Intercontinental Burswood Resort
Great Eastern Highway, Bur-
swood; tel: 08-9362 7777, toll-
free: 1800-999 667; www.
burswood.intercontinental.com;
$$$$; bus: 24, 296
Riverside location 3km (2
miles) east of the city centre.
Spectacular buildings with
luxurious accommodation
are part of a complex with
an 18-hole golf course, the-
atre, state tennis centre and
the only casino in WA, open
24 hours. If you are feeling
like really showing off, you

Above: having a pint in the M Cafe at The Melbourne.

can also arrive by helicopter:
the resort has its own pad,
chopper and pilot. Recently
the complex has been refur-
bished and has had a push
at upgrading its eating
options – fine-dining Chi-
nese at **Yu** is excellent and
the funky and awfully spelt
A(LURE) is also worth a meal
or drink at the bar.
SEE ALSO RESTAURANTS, P.104

Mont Clare Boutique Apartments
190 Hay Street; tel: 08-9224
4300; www.montclare
apartments.com; $$; bus: red
CAT; map p.135 C1

Near the Swan River, these
stylish and bright apartments
are in a good location, well
served by local restaurants.
Well-furnished apartments in
a choice of sizes, with a full
kitchen and laundry, outdoor
pool and gym.

Regal Apartments
11 Regal Place; tel: 08-9221
8614, toll-free: 1800-778 614;
www.regalapartments.com.au;
$$; bus: red CAT; map p.135 D2
Apartments sleeping up to
seven, so ideal for families or
groups, with a fully equipped
kitchen and laundry.

Northbridge

Nomads Billabong Backpackers Resort
381 Beaufort Street; tel: 08-
9328 7720; www.billabong
resort.com.au; $; bus: 60, 67;
map p.134 B4
Adjacent to Northbridge

Be aware that in Australia a sign
saying 'hotel' can simply mean
a pub and is not necessarily an
indication of accommodation,
especially where grand old
properties are concerned. It
dates from the days when all
pubs had rooms for rent and
were often the only accommo-
dation to be found in a town.

Below: in the bar at Rydges.

entertainment and restaurant area, this colourful and lively hostel boasts air-conditioning and modern facilities, a swimming pool and gym, as well as a free breakfast.

The Old Swan Barracks
6 Francis Street; tel: 08-9428 0000; www.theoldswan barracks.com; $; train: Perth; map p.134 B3

A backpackers' hostel that's close to Cultural Centre, art gallery and museum and the Northbridge entertainment and restaurant area. Many facilities, including a pool table, kitchen and gym.

Pension of Perth
3 Throssell Street; tel: 08-9228 9049; www.pensionperth.com. au; $$; bus: 60

Quiet 1897-built 'federation' style home near Hyde Park; seven master bedrooms with en suite (spa or bath), fine furnishings and French antiques.

Silver-service breakfast is served in the lounge or by the swimming pool.

SEE ALSO GAY AND LESBIAN, P.62

Quest West End
451 Murray Street; tel: 08-9480 3888, toll-free: 1800-334 033; www.questwestend.com.au; $$$; bus: red CAT; map p.133 E3

At border of the CBD and main shopping areas, with easy access to the restaurants and entertainments of Hay Street, Murray Street and Northbridge, this offers modern apartments with full kitchens and an on-site gym. Part of a larger Quest chain, which is always reliable.

The Witch's Hat
148 Palmerston Street; tel: 08-9228 4228; www.witchs hat.com; $; bus: 60, 67; map p.134 A4

Off Russell Square in a quirky, historic 1897 town house that was restored in 1998. Very pleasant and popular, with light, large rooms. It gets its quirky name from the turret-style point on the house.

Subiaco

King's Park Motel
255 Thomas Street; tel: 08-9381 0000, toll-free: 1800-655 362; www.kingsparkmotel.com.au; $; bus: 103; map p.132 B1

Facing Kings Park on the road leading to the University of WA, this offers single, double, triple or family rooms, some with cooking facilities. All have a handy fridge, and fun facilities such as a pool and barbecue area are available.

Quest Subiaco
222 Hay Street; tel: 08-9380 0800, toll-free: 1800-628 788; www.questsubiaco.com.au; $$$; train: Subiaco; map p.132 C3

Left: fairy-tale meets backpacker at The Witch's Hat.

Left: internet access is often offered at backpackers' hostels.

Accommodation in Perth's hotels is the tightest market in Australia at the moment, so don't wait until you get there to try and get a room. Make sure you book ahead, unless you are happy to try your luck at backpackers' if you don't have any joy at the city's larger hotels.

In cosmopolitan Subiaco with boutique shops, interesting restaurants and bars, and the Regal Theatre nearby. The apartments have full kitchens and laundry facilities; an outdoor pool, spa and barbecues are also at your disposal. The Vic bar and restaurant is part of the complex. It is also within spitting distance of Subiaco Oval, so when there is a game of AFL or rugby on you will be in the centre of it, but be warned, the queue to get into the pub will stretch down the road.

Fremantle

Esplanade
Marine Terrace/Essex Street; tel: 08-9432 4000, toll-free: 1800-998 201; www.esplanadehotel fremantle.com.au; $$$$; train: Fremantle
Elegant gold rush-era building with atrium, two pools,

Price categories are for a standard double room per night without breakfast.
$$$$ = A$250 plus
$$$ = A$175–$250
$$ = A$100–$175
$ = under A$100

three spas, fitness centre, bar and two restaurants. Most rooms have private balconies with views overlooking popular parklands, tropical gardens and pools. Across Marine Terrace lawns is Fishing Boat Harbour, with restaurants and entertainment.

Freo Mews
111 South Terrace; tel: 08-9336 6379; $$; train: Fremantle
Elegant apartments for up to six people in two-storey mews houses. Comfortable, with good amenities and central for all Fremantle attractions.

Kilkelly's B&B
82 Marine Terrace; tel: 08-9336 1744; www.wt.com.au/~kilkelly; $$; train: Fremantle
Located in a renovated 1883 mariner's cottage opposite Fishing Boat Harbour. Stroll easily from here to tourist attractions, restaurants, markets and shops. Rooms open onto an upper veranda.

Pier 21 Resort
7–9 John Street; tel: 08-9336 2555; www.pier21resort. com.au; $$; train: North Fremantle
On the banks of the Swan, fully serviced one- and two-bed apartments with kitchens and river views. Indoor and

outdoor pools overlook the river marina; there are also two spas, tennis and squash courts and a barbecue area.

Port Mill
3/17 Essex Street; tel: 08-9433 3832; www.babs.com.au/ portmill; $$; train: Fremantle
Heritage building in the heart of Fremantle, decorated in modern French style with a Freo twist. Three luxury rooms with wrought-iron balconies overlooking a gorgeous courtyard are available for a romantic experience.

Cottesloe, Claremont, Swanbourne and Scarborough

Cottesloe Beach Chalets
6 John Street, Cottesloe; tel: 08-9383 5000; www.cottesloe beachchalets.com.au; $$; train: Cottesloe
Just off the oceanfront Marine Parade, these self-contained chalets sleep up to five, with full cooking facilities and laundry available. There is also an on-site pool and barbecue. The nearby pub is a favourite with younger patrons.

The Dunes
15 Filburn Street, Scarborough; tel: 08-9245 2797; www.inter leaf.ie/dunes; $$; bus: 400
Set back from the West Coast Highway in Scarborough, but close to the beach and local facilities. Modern, well-appointed two-bed

units with full kitchens and laundry; there is also a private courtyard with barbecue facilities.

Hillary's Harbour Resort Apartments

68 Southside Drive, Hillary's Boat Harbour; tel: 08-9262 7888, toll-free: 1800-240 078; www.hillarysresort.com.au; $$; train: Warwick, then taxi

Harbourside one, two and three-bed modern units on Sorrento Quay boardwalk, with views across the marina; all come with a full kitchen and laundry. There is also a pool, spa and sauna and barbecue area.

Mosman Beach Apartments

3 Fairlight Street, Mosman Park; tel: 08-9285 6400; www.mosmanbeach.com; $$; train: Mosman Park

Between Perth and Fremantle, this range of apartments

are just 300m/yds from the beach and located in a tropical garden setting. There is a heated pool, barbecue area and gym. Great for family groups who aren't too fussy and want to be close to the ocean at a reasonable price.

Ocean Beach Hotel

Eric Street/Marine Parade, Cottesloe; tel: 08-9384 2555; www.obh.com.au; $$; train: Cottesloe

Overlooking the Indian Ocean, this place is right on the beach and ideal for those who want to chill out on the sand and do some surfing. Recently refurbished, it is modern and lively, with a seafront restaurant, café, pizza-bar and two bars heavily used by younger clientele.

Ocean Villas

17–19 Hastings Street; tel: 08-9245 1066; www.oceanvillas.com.au; $$; bus: 400

One road away from the busy West Coast Highway and a two-minute walk to the beach, shops, restaurants, bars and Observation City hotel facilities. Villas each have private courtyards and all are three-bedroomed to

sleep five people. They have full cooking and laundry facilities, and there's a spa on site.

Rendezvous Observation City Hotel

The Esplanade; tel: 08-9245 1000; www.rendezvoushotels.com; $$$; bus: 400

Luxury hotel on the beach, a rare example here of a high-rise building on the coast. Wide-ranging facilities include several restaurants and bars, nightclub, pool, spa, tennis courts and gym. The rooms have had a recent refurbishment, but the pool area is still sporting '80s-style fake rocks and waterfalls.

Sorrento Beach Resort

1 Padbury Circle; tel: 08-9246 8100, toll-free: 1800-998 484; www.sorrentobeach.com.au; $$; train: Warwick, then taxi

Metres from the beach in Sorrento and facing Hillary's Boat Harbour, so handy for the local restaurants, bars, shops, ferry to Rottnest and the AQWA aquarium experience. The resort has an outdoor pool, spa, sauna and barbecue. Hotel-style studio apartments have two or three beds with kitchens.

Sunmoon Resort

Price categories are for a standard double room per night without breakfast.
$$$$ = A$250 plus
$$$ = A$175–$250
$$ = A$100–$175
$ = under A$100

Left: the Rendezvous Observation City Hotel at Scarborough.

200 West Coast Highway; tel: 08-9245 8000, toll-free: 1800-090 054; www.sunmoon.com.au; $$; bus: 400

Close to the beach, restaurants and entertainment. Hotel rooms, studio apartments and two- or three-bed units decorated in a distinctly Asian style. Tropical gardens with pool and Café Eclipse, a restaurant serving Australasian cuisine.

Swan Valley and the Perth Hills

Carmelot Bed and Breakfast
145 Carmel Road, Carmel; tel: 08-9293 5150; www.members. westnet.com.au/smithers/ carmelot/index.html; $; by car

A sense of humour pervades this B&B, with three medieval-themed rooms: King Arthur, Lancelot and Guinevere (with a four-poster, canopied bed). There is a sword set in a stone in the gardens of Carmelot, which is surrounded by orchards and just five minutes from Kalamunda History Village. Also has swimming pool, spa and barbecue. All rooms are en suite, and the tariff includes a full cooked breakfast, afternoon tea and a newspaper.

The Loose Box
6825 Great Eastern Highway, Mundaring; tel: 08-9295 1787; www.loosebox.com.au; $$$$; by car

This fabulous French restaurant also has its own boutique cottages on the property. The idea is that you eat at the restaurant and then stay overnight, and some packages include a dégustation meal in the price.

Mundaring Weir Hotel
Mundaring Weir Road, Mundaring; tel: 08-9295 1106; www.mundaringweir hotel.com.au; $; by car

This historic Weir-area hotel is surrounded by jarrah forest and is very popular as a centre for walkers using the many local trails. Eleven modern units overlook the forest, or pool and amphitheatre area, where open-air concerts are held in the summer months and kangaroos roam in the evenings. Rooms have open wood fires and good facilities.

Novotel Vines Resort
Verdelho Drive, Upper Swan; tel: 08-9297 3000, toll-free: 1300-656 565; www.novotelvines. com.au; $$$; by car

Luxury resort and country club noted for its 36-hole championship golf course. Accommodation includes rooms with two double beds, suites with lounges, or self-contained two- or three-bedroom apartments. Restaurants and bars, pool, spa, gym, tennis and squash courts on site.

Swan Valley Fauntleroy House B&B
4 James Street, Guildford; tel: 08-9379 0270; www.fauntleroy house.com.au; $$; by car

This restored 1902 house

Perth Airport is undergoing renovation and expansion, announcing a A$1 billion package which will see new regional, domestic and international facilities built over five to seven years. A new airport hotel is also part of the plan, which will help with hotel capacity in Perth, especially for passengers in transit.

has three spacious en suite rooms, decorated with antique furniture. There is also a comfortable guest lounge. The Rose Suite has a four-poster bed, and two rooms open onto the veranda with views over garden and pool. Continental breakfast included, but a cooked one is also available.

Swan Valley Oasis Resort
10250 West Swan Road; tel: 08-9296 5555; www.swanvalley oasis.com; $$; by car

Set in tropical gardens on 22 hectares (55 acres) by the Swan River, with spa rooms. A luxury self-contained double apartment with kitchen and laundry is also available. The resort has a heated pool and spa, gym, sauna and laundry, and a fully licensed restaurant. You can also play Supa Golf here, with oversized clubs and balls.

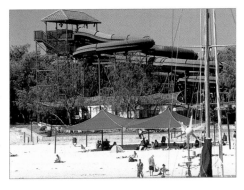

Right: Hillary's Boat Harbour, a good area to stay in when travelling with children.

73

Literature

Western Australia is no stranger to the creative arts, and many say that the city's isolation is responsible for its thriving writing scene. Perth and Western Australia can be proud of its literary culture, boasting several important Australian authors, such as Elizabeth Jolley and Tim Winton, who have immortalised the local life and landscapes in the national consciousness. There are a number of good bookshops here, too, in particular some interesting places to pick up second-hand tomes. Book clubs are popular, too; you will be met with surprise if you can't lay claim to be currently reading something.

Authors

Elizabeth Jolley

Jolley (1923–2007) was born in England and raised in a German-speaking household, but immigrated to WA in 1959, and Perth is happy to claim her as its own. It wasn't until she was in her 50s that she received literary acclaim, but she subsequently won Melbourne's *The Age* newspaper 'Book of the Year' award three times (for *Mr Scobie's Riddle*, *My Father's Moon* and *The Georges' Wife*), as well as the Miles Franklin prize for *The Well*, while her non-fiction title *Central Mischief* was awarded the WA Premier's Prize in 1993.

Tim Winton

Winton (1960–) was born in WA and still lives here today. He is considered one of Australia's top contemporary authors and began one of his classic titles, *An Open Swimmer*, when he was 19. The book went on to win the Australian/Vogel National Literary Award. Tim is a prolific writer, with many of his novels set in the landscapes of WA. He has also written teenage fic-

Above: author Elizabeth Jolley.

tion. *Lockie Leonard, Human Torpedo* won the WA Premier's Award for children's fiction and has been adapted into a stage play. Tim has been named a Living Treasure by the National Trust, and awarded the Centenary Medal for service to literature and the community.

Other Significant Authors

Kim Scott was the first Indigenous writer to win the Miles Franklin Literary Award (*Benang*, 2000). Sally Morgan's book *My Place* is an Australian classic. A.B. Facey's autobiographical work, *A Fortunate Life*, has

given voice to the early days of Australia, and T.A.G. Hungerford's collection of autobiographical stories in *Straight Shooter* has become a classic voice of Australian character.

Bookshops

Boffins

806 Hay Street; tel: 08-9321 5755; www.boffinsbookshop. com.au; Mon–Sat 9am–5.30pm, Fri until 8pm, Sun noon–5pm; train: Perth; map p.134 A2
Excellent bookshop specialising in technical and specialist books across all subjects.

Bookcaffe

137 Claremont Crescent, Swanbourne; tel: 08-9385 0553; www.bookcaffe.com.au; Mon–Sat 9am–6pm; train: Swanbourne
Relax with a coffee and peruse the latest titles.

Borders

625–635 Hay Street, Perth; tel: 08-9325 6655; www.borders. com.au; Mon–Thur 8.30am–7pm, Fri until 9pm, Sat 9am–5pm, Sun noon–6pm; train: Perth; map p.134 A2
You won't need any introduction to the giant Borders chain,

Left: enticing displays at Elizabeth's Secondhand Bookshop.

busy, and you are welcome to sit down and browse.

Oxford Street Books
131 Oxford Street, Leederville; tel: 08-9443 9844; daily 10am–late; train: Leederville
A small, quirky bookstore with lots of travel, photography, women's studies and children's books. Good selection of fiction, too.

Planet Books
642–648 Beaufort Street, Mount Lawley; tel: 08-9328 7464; bus: 21, 60; daily 10am–10pm
Next to the immensely popular Planet Video (which rents videos but also sells a huge range of music, scripts, concert tickets and more), is Planet Books, which sells a quirky range of texts, from humorous cultural observational texts to cookbooks, health texts and more. You are encouraged to browse, sit and read before buying. The staff are friendly, and the large chandelier in the store sets the mood for fun. You can also buy small gifts such as magnets and cards.

Reading list
A Fortunate Life, A.B. Facey (UWA Press)
Cloudstreet, Tim Winton (Penguin, Australia)
Dirt Music, Tim Winton (Picador)
My Place, Sally Morgan (Fremantle Press)

As part of the **Perth International Arts Festival** *(see p.54)*, the Perth Writers Festival happens over three days in February. The festival includes visiting authors, workshops, debate and much more.

---

but Perth has only recently been treated to a store, and it has been met with enthusiasm. If you're looking for popular texts you're likely to find the cheapest price here.

Elizabeth's Secondhand Bookshop
820 Hay Street, Perth; tel: 08-9481 8848; www.elizabeths bookshop.com.au; Mon–Thur 9am–6pm, Fri until 8pm, Sat until 5pm, Sun noon–5pm; train: Perth; map p.134 A2
This chain of second-hand bookshops started in the

early 70s, and stocks a large range of all types of literature, from fiction to self-help, coffee-table and children's books and magazines. Books are reasonably priced, but vary in quality. A credit system operates whereby if you take in books to sell you receive a credit amount to spend at the store. When you have read the books, you can return them for more credit.

New Edition
82 High Street, Fremantle; tel: 08-9335 2383; www.new edition.com.au; daily 10am–5pm, Thur until 9pm; train: Fremantle
A great bookshop with good coffee-table books at the front of the store, lots of political science and a good children's section. Always

---

Local publishers include Fremantle Press, which was established in 1976, with the aim of developing the widest possible audience for outstanding Western Australian writers and artists. Also prolific in publishing local titles is the University of Western Australia Press.

Below: a fun place to visit for buying books and more.

Museums and Galleries

Spend some time discovering the cultural and historical side of Perth and Western Australia. The Cultural Centre between the CBD and Northbridge is the natural first stop, but Fremantle also offers some fascinating clues into the area's maritime history. From the intriguing, large Aboriginal art collection at the Art Gallery of Western Australia, to the blue whale skeleton at the WA Museum, you will find many exhibits offering different ways to connect to this unusual land.

City Centre

Art Gallery of Western Australia

47 James Street; tel: 08-9492 6600; www.artgallery.wa. gov.au; daily 10am–5pm; free (temporary exhibitions may charge entry); train: Perth; map p.134 B3

Several floors of modern, well-lit galleries display more than 1,000 works of art, including Australian and international paintings, sculpture, prints, crafts and decorative arts. On the first floor of the main building, two galleries house one of the continent's best collections of Aboriginal art *(see also p.27)*. Also part of the Art Gallery of WA and worth seeing are the **Centenary Galleries**, contained in the former Perth Police Court building. Ask at the front desk to be shown the short cut through to the galleries. Among the highlights here are several paintings from the important Heidelberg School of artists: *Down on His Luck* by Fred McCubbin, *Breaking the News* by John Longstaff, *Ada Furlong* by Tom Roberts, *Black Thursday* by William Strutt and *Hillside* by Arthur Streeton.

Almost as intriguing as the art is the building itself, a late 19th-century interpretation of French Renaissance style. It was unusual for Perth architecture, but localised in its use of WA materials like the pink Donnybrook stone of the facades, hard jarrah timber for floors and interior furnishings, stained-glass feature panels and Australian-made ornate pressed-metal ceilings. The

Below: Gerhard Marks's *The Caller (left)* stands in the grounds of the Art Gallery of WA *(right)*.

Left: the International Gallery at the Art Gallery of WA.

courts closed in 1982. One courtroom and two adjoining cells are preserved.

There are regular, free public tours of the gallery (Tue–Fri, Sun 1pm, plus a special one focusing on a specific work at 12.30pm on Fri). One painting that is almost always included on the general tour is *The Foundation of Perth*, by George Pitt, depicting the moment when Mrs Dance marked the founding of Perth by attacking a tree with an axe.

Just outside the Art Gallery is a dramatic steel sculpture, *Between*, by Clement Meadmore, and, near the pool, another startling artwork, *The Caller*, by Gerhard Marks.

Perth Institute of Contemporary Art

51 James Street; tel: 08-9227 6144; www.pica.org.au; Mon–Fri 10am–6pm, gallery Tue–Sun 11am–6pm; free; train: Perth; map p.134 B3

The PICA building was a school once upon a time, but is now home to Perth's main contemporary art spaces. The soaring main gallery has studios on a mezzanine, and there's a bar and café and a performance theatre on the ground floor. Sharing space with Performing Arts Centre Society **(PACS)** are the **Photographers Gallery**, **WA Actors Centre** and **Impressions Gallery**, which exhibits prints. **Artrage**, Perth's alternative arts coordinator, is around the corner. There is usually some contemporary art on show at PICA – photography, installations, large-scale graphic work and audiovisual media are just some of what you can expect.

Northbridge

Western Australian Museum

Perth Cultural Centre, James Street; tel: 08-9212 3700; www.museum.wa.gov.au; daily 9.30am–5pm; free; train: Perth; map p.134 B3

Set in an elegant red-brick and sandstone building with a colonnaded upper floor, the collections and research at the WA Museum are centred on systematics, ecology, biogeography, as well as the evolution of living and fossil organisms, palaeontology, mineralogy, meteoritics, anthropology and archaeology, history, maritime history, maritime archaeology and conservation. As some of the oldest land on earth is found in WA, scientists have access to its earliest life forms, and a wealth of artefacts of early man, such as the rock paintings in the Pilbara.

In 1999 a fossil proving the earliest evidence of life on earth was discovered in WA's Pilbara region. Now on display in the Dinosaur Gallery, it looks like a slab of red rock. It holds the oldest life-fossil known, stromatolites estimated to be 3.5 billion years old. Living versions still grow in the highly saline water of Hamelin Pool at Shark Bay, far north of WA.

Australia began taking on its present-day form 120 million years ago, when the

---

One of Western Australia's oldest and wealthiest families are the Holmes à Courts, and they certainly own an impressive art collection. If you are in Margaret River, visit Vasse Felix winery (which the family owns), where you'll not only find modern sculpture in the gardens, but a large Aboriginal art collection inside. In Perth you can visit the Holmes à Court Gallery at level 1, 11 Brown Street in East Perth. The gallery is the passion of Janet Holmes à Court, and its aim is to present exhibitions that 'examine the diversity and strengths of the Holmes à Court Collection'. The collection is impressive and worth a look if you are in the area. See www.holmesacourt gallery.com.au.

ition of 1827, including a complete original courtroom, a pedal radio that kept out-back families in touch, a complete 1917 pharmacy, clothes, toys and furniture.

Fremantle

Fremantle History Museum

1 Finnerty Street; tel: 08-9430 7966; Mon–Fri 10am–4.30pm, Sat 1–5pm, Sun 10.30am–4.30pm; entry by donation; train: Fremantle

The former asylum building is one of Fremantle's most significant landmarks. It now houses the Fremantle History Museum – a museum of the social history of Western Australia. Free tours of the building, with its fascinating history and 'resident ghost', are conducted daily. The grounds are beautiful and at weekends you'll often discover music being played in the courtyard. There is also a small shop selling WA art, crafts, books and more.

Maritime Museum

Victoria Quay; tel: 08-9431 8444; www.mm.wa.gov.au/maritime; daily 9.30am–5pm; admission charge; train: Fremantle

Fremantle has been the setting for key phases in Western Australia's history, many of them connected with the sea, making it a fitting setting for the Maritime Museum, which opened on Victoria Quay in 2002. Just a few hundred metres along the waterfront is Arthur Head, where Captain Fremantle planted the Union flag and claimed WA for Britain in 1829. The safe anchorage made the colony essential to naval traffic and trade for

A new world-class museum for WA will be built on the site of the former East Perth Power Station (near Claisebrook train station). If you go past the building at the moment, it looks like a huge, ramshackle shed, but great things are planned. The museum will cost A$500 million to build, and will show the state's history, indigenous heritage, unique environment, sporting greats, inventors, as well as stories of WA's people, from Aboriginal people through to leading doctors, teachers and miners. The WA Museum's team of scientists have collectively discovered more than 1,000 new species, including 47 new species of animal from 2007 to 2008. Planning and design began in 2008, with construction expected to begin in 2012. The project is expected to be completed in late 2015.

supercontinent Gondwana began to break up, separating South America, Africa, Madagascar and India from Australia. South America was connected to Australia at its southern tip, via an ice-free Antarctica, until 30 million years ago.

Isolated since then, Australia's prehistoric life forms were undisturbed and safe from man until perhaps 50,000–40,000 BC. Botanists believe Australia was the prime location of early flowering-plant evolution. Some of the weird and wonderful products of isolation survive, such as the duck-billed platypus, kangaroo and wallaby.

The museum has a pleasant coffee shop next to the Old Gaol, built by convicts in 1855–6 and now crammed with memorabilia of Perth life since James Stirling's exped-

more than a century, and it was the first sight of Australia for thousands of hopeful migrants until well into the 20th century. Wartime service turned the port into the biggest Allied submarine base outside Pearl Harbor.

The museum covers everything from whaling, pearling, fishing and trade to immigration, recreation and globalisation. There are many delightful details to be discovered along the way, such as the importation of the Mediterranean 'blessing of the sea' festival, introduced to WA by Sicilian fishermen.

From here you can also tour a decommissioned submarine, HMAS *Ovens*. There is a joint ticket for both the museum and a submarine tour, or you can just take the submarine tour. Ticket sales are from the Maritime Museum, with tours running throughout the day.

Motor Museum
B Shed, Victoria Quay; tel: 08-9336 5222; www.fremantle motormuseum.net; Mon–Sun 9.30am–5pm; admission charge; train: Fremantle
From the basis of Peter Briggs's family collection, this museum for the motor enthusiast features exhibits of world land-speed record-breakers such as historic racing cars, including Formula One champion Allan Jones's world-beating Williams, more than 50 motorcycles, and the Aston Martin V8 Volante used by James Bond in *The Living Daylights*. Cars range in age from an 1886 motorised tricycle replica to a 1986 'funny

car', a type of drag-racing car which has a recorded top speed of 379kmh (235.47mph).

Shipwreck Galleries
Cliff Street; tel: 08-9431 8444; www.museum.wa.gov.au/ maritime/swg.asp; daily 9.30am–5pm; free but donations welcome, admission fees for special exhibits may apply; train: Fremantle
Considered the foremost maritime archaeology museum in the southern hemisphere, the Shipwreck Galleries' star exhibit is the stern of the *Batavia*, a Dutch ship wrecked off the Abrolhos islands in 1629, with a famous history. Part of a Dutch expedition to the East Indies, it became separated from its companion

ships on 4 June 1629, when it struck a reef. The crew escaped to two small islands, with provisions and treasure, but little water. While the captain, François Pelsart, and a few other men set off to find help, the ship's officer Jerome Cornelisz mutinied, leading to a bloodbath among the remaining crew.

In September, Pelsart returned. The mutineers were put to death, apart from two, who were marooned near Champion Bay to become the first-known white inhabitants of the continent. Nothing was heard of them again.

The *Batavia* was raised from the depths by marine archaeologists between 1972 and 1976.

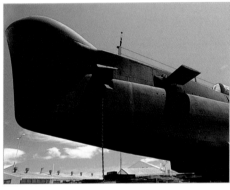

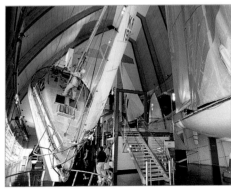

Right: HMAS *Ovens* submarine *(top)* and the *Parry Endeavour* yacht *(bottom)* in which Jon Sanders sailed solo around the world in the 1980s, on display at the Maritime Museum.

Music and Dance

Music is a large part of Perth's social scene, and crowds turn out in their thousands for open-air concerts in the summer months. Today, Perth is a more popular tour stop than it used to be, and artists such as Elton John, Kanye West and Rod Stewart have recently come to town. Meanhile, national classical symphony orchestras frequently visit Perth, including the Australian Chamber Orchestra and the Australian String Quartet. For further listings of music venues, see *Nightlife, p.85,* and *Pubs and Bars, p.96–9.*

Music

CLASSICAL

His Majesty's Theatre
825 Hay Street; tel: 08-9484 1133; www.hismajestys theatre.com.au; train: Perth; map p.134 A2
A beautiful, ornate Victorian theatre used for all types of concerts, theatre and stand-up comedy.

Perth Concert Hall
5 St Georges Terrace; tel: 08-9231 9900; www.perthconcert hall.com.au; train: Perth; map p.134 B1
Perth's principal classical music auditorium is home to the Western Australian Symphony Orchestra (WASO). The Concert Hall also has a huge pipe organ behind the stage, forming a significant part of the rear wall.

West Australian Opera
Concerts are held at various locations; tel: 08-9278 8999; www.waopera.asn.au; bookings tel: 08-9484 1144; www.bocticketing.com.au
The West Australian Opera company enjoys a strong fol-

lowing and a talented cast. Classic productions such as *Aida*, *The Barber of Seville* and *The Magic Flute* keep audiences enthralled. The company also has a young artists' programme, where they identify key young performers and run a series of short concerts to show their abilities.

Western Australian Symphony Orchestra
445 Hay Street; tel: 08-9326 0000; www.waso.com.au; train: Perth; map p.134 B2
WASO has recently appointed Paul Daniel to be its principal conductor as of 2009. Daniel was music director at the English National Opera from 1997 to 2005 and has guest conducted with major orchestras around the world, including the London Philharmonic, Philharmonia, the Royal Philharmonic, the

Right: the ornate facade of His Majesty's Theatre.

Left: Perth has a thriving live music scene.

itional and mainstream jazz.

Perth Jazz Society
509 Charles Street, North Perth; tel: 08-9444 1051; www.perth jazzsociety.com; bus: 400; admission charge

Held at the Charles Hotel on Monday nights from 8pm, Perth Jazz Society presents a range of excellent artists, both local and international. Founded in 1973, it is a not-for-profit association.

Universal Bar
221 William Street, Northbridge; tel: 08-9227 6771; daily lunch–late; free; train: Perth; map p.134 A3

One of Perth's most popular jazz/swing bands is Libby Hammer's Hip Mo' Toast. Hip Mo' Toast performs here regularly.

CONTEMPORARY
Western Australia produces even more exponents of rock and pop than jazz; there are live sounds somewhere almost every night. Musically, Perth has always had a thriving local scene with links to

New York Philharmonic and many orchestras throughout Europe. The WASO's programme is always wide and varied, and recently the orchestra has started to venture into some contemporary pairings when visiting musicians call in to Perth. These concerts often take place in Kings Park during summer.

JAZZ
Perth has nurtured an outstanding line-up of talented local jazz musicians, and the pool spreads every year because of the internationally respected Conservatorium at **West Australian Academy of Performing Arts (WAAPA)**. Graduates form many of the groups playing in venues across Perth. Also, Australian and international musos make regular visits to the west, often at the invitation of the **Perth Jazz Society (PJS)**. Lucky Oceans and Rick Steele are the biggest jazz exports from Perth.

The Jazz Cellar
Cnr Scarborough Beach and Buxton roads, Mount Hawthorn;

tel: 08-9447 8111; www.all aboutjazz.com; bus: 15; Fri 7pm; admission charge

Through the quirky entrance, which is a red phone box, and down the stairs for the most intimate of jazz venues; Fri night only. You can BYO food and drinks.

Jazz Picnic
Jabe Dodd Park, Mosman; summer: third Sun of every month noon–4pm; free; train: Mosman Park

Open-air jazz picnic.

The Navy Club
64 High Street, Fremantle; tel: 08-9335 3015; www.media highway.com.au/jazzfremantle; Sun 4–7pm; admission charge; train: Fremantle

Jazz Fremantle meets at The Navy Club every Sunday. Trad-

The Jazz Line (tel: 08-9357 2807) has a complete rundown of current venues and events. **Perth Jazz Club** holds traditional jazz nights at various locations around Perth on Tuesday nights. For current listings visit: www.jazzwa.com/ jazzclubofwa.

Below: jazz is performed in many types of venues; here, at Friends Restaurant *(see p.103)*.

Left: West Australian Ballet dancers rehearse for the production of *Obsession* at His Majesty's Theatre.

cultural music and dance, especially world music. Open for classes and specific shows only.

Mustang Bar
46 Lake Street, Northbridge; tel: 08-9328 2350; www.mustang bar.com.au; train: Perth; map p.134 A3
A favourite with the rockabilly set, you can catch some good tunes and jiving here.

The Rosemount Hotel
459 Fitzgerald Street, North Perth; tel: 08-9328 7062; www.rosemounthotel.com.au; admission only on band nights; bus: 19, 400
A great spot to catch local rock bands when they're back in town from touring.

MUSIC SHOPS
78 Records
914 Hay Street; tel: 08-9322 6384; Mon–Sat 9am–6pm, Fri until 9pm, Sun noon–5pm; train: Perth; map p.133 E2
Has a huge amount of stock – if you can't find it elsewhere, you'll find it here.

Urban Records
117 Oxford Street, Leederville; tel: 08-9201 2500; daily 10am–late; train: Leederville
This record store has a good mix of contemporary music, from club to rock to world. Walk through, and at the rear you'll find a quirky clothing and gift shop.

Wesley Classics
Shop 4, Arcade 800, 800 Hay Street; tel: 08-9321 1978; www.wesleyclassics.com.au; Mon–Sat 10am–6pm, Fri until 8pm; train: Perth; map p.134 A2
A fantastic CD store for classical music-lovers. They can source widely and are happy to order in for you.

some of the most iconic bands in Australian history, such as INXS and AC/DC. AC/DC's original front man Bon Scott, who grew up in Western Australia, is buried in Fremantle Cemetery.

Perth's booming music scene, known in some circles as 'the new Seattle', is largely thanks to the recent success of bands such as Eskimo Joe, The Waifs, John Butler Trio, Little Birdy, Jebediah, the Sleepy Jackson, The Panics, End of Fashion and Gyroscope. To recognise the thriving local industry, there is an annual awards, called the WAMis (West Australian Music Industry), recognising talents in the industry. These awards are promoted nationally through Triple J Radio (http://triplej.abc.net.au,

99.3FM in Perth).
Fly by Night Musicians Club
1 Holdsworth Street (entry off Parry Street), Fremantle; tel: 08-9430 5976; www.flybynight.org; admission charge; train: Fremantle
The Fly by Night Musicians Club is a not-for-profit community musicians' club and music venue and today is probably Perth's most serious music venue. Some of WA's biggest bands, including the John Butler Trio, The Waifs, Eskimo Joe and The Panics, started off their careers at the club. Worth checking out.

Kulcha
1st floor, 13 South Terrace, Fremantle; tel: 08-9336 4544; www.kulcha.com.au; admission charge; train: Fremantle
Kulcha's focus is on multi-

Left: browsing records at one of Perth's stores.

youth, teachers, families and communities each year.

Gilkison Dance Studio
45 Murray Street; tel: 08-9325 6566; www.gilkisons.com.au; train: Perth; map p.134 B2
If you've got some time in Perth, enrol for a series of classes at Gilkison's. Lessons include cha-cha, waltz, jive, tango, samba and more.

The Irish Club
61 Townshend Road, Subiaco; tel: 08-9381 5213; train: Subiaco; map p.132 B3
Irish music lessons and set dancing from 8pm, Mondays.

Dance

CLASSICAL

West Australian Ballet
Level 2, His Majesty's Theatre, 625 Hay Street; tel: 08-9214 0707; www.waballet.com.au; train: Perth; map p.134 A2
In 1952, West Australian Ballet, the first ballet company in Australia, was established by Madame Kira Bousloff.

West Australian Ballet stages everything from full-length classical ballets and narrative ballets to shorter works, and encompasses a variety of choreographic styles. West Australian Ballet also tours nationally and internationally, as well as conducting regional tours in Western Australia.

Madame Bousloff, who founded West Australian Ballet, was a Prima Ballerina with the Ballets Russes and travelled to the east coast of Australia in 1938. After completing her commitment with the Ballets Russes she travelled west to Perth on holiday and fell in love with the city, declaring that the beautiful coastline reminded her of the French Riviera.

CONTEMPORARY

Buzz Dance Theatre
King Street Arts Centre, 357–365 Murray Street; tel: 08-9226 2322; www.buzzdance.com.au; train: Perth; map p.134 A2
Buzz Dance Theatre was founded in 1985 and is a leading company for children and youth dance. They are heavily involved at school level, tour nationally and internationally, and come into contact with over 20,000

STEPS Youth Dance Company
Level 1, King Street Arts Centre, 357–365 Murray Street; tel: 08-9226 2133; www.stepsyouth dance.com.au; train: Perth; map p.134 A2
Another youth dance group, STEPS was founded in 1988 and has a focus on dance relevant to young people, and to assisting young dancers in working together and in performance.

Below: West Australian Ballet founder, Madame Bousloff.

Nightlife

If you expect Perth to be up until the wee hours on a Tuesday night, think again. The clubbing scene is very much limited to the weekend, the biggest nights for going out being Saturday and Sunday. In the week, locals are more likely to head out for dinner and a quiet drink at the pub, so if you want to party with your fellow man, it is best to aim for the high-ticket weekend nights, when clubs stay open until 4–5am and most of the population are willing to nurse a hangover the next day. Alternatively, for some evening entertainment mid-week, hit the Burswood Casino or one of the comedy nights on offer.

Casino

Burswood Casino
Great Eastern Highway, Burswood; tel: 08-9362 7777; www.burswood.com.au/casino; daily 24 hours; admission charge; bus: 37

WA's only casino is open 24 hours in the Burswood Entertainment Complex, with nine restaurants and six bars. There is a dress code of no jeans, vests, thongs (flip-flops) or sneakers. However, once you're inside you'll wonder who was in charge of enforcing dress standards. There is an international room which is only for high rollers, and there are always a smattering of Ferraris, Maseratis and Porches parked out in front.

Comedy

Comedy Lounge
The Charles Hotel, 509 Charles Street, North Perth; tel: 08-9309 1139; www.comedylounge.com.au; shows: Thur 7pm; admission charge; bus: 19, 346

Comedy Lounge brings local, interstate and international acts to Perth. There is usually a Thursday night gig which runs for a couple of hours.

The Laugh Resort
The Brass Monkey, Cnr William and James streets, Northbridge; shows: Wed 8pm; admission charge; train: Perth; map p.134 A3

Held every Wednesday night at The Brass Monkey pub, The Laugh Resort is a place to spy local stand-up comedians. There's also an

opportunity to test your own humour, as they offer open mic, too.

Lazy Susan's Comedy Den
Brisbane Hotel, Cnr Brisbane and Beaufort streets, Highgate; tel: 08-9328 2543; bookings through BOCS: 08-9484 1133; www.lazysusans.com.au; shows: Fri 8pm; admission charge; bus: 60; map p.134 B4

Every Friday night is stand-up night. Also opens for special events.

Food

Sadly, late-night food options are scarce in Perth, especially if you want something other than fast food.

Cosmos Kebabs
129 Oxford Street, Leederville; tel: 08-9444 8429; daily 10am–3am; train: Leederville

If you've been dancing up a storm at one of Leederville's pubs or clubs, then Cosmos is a required pit stop. Cosmos specialises in shish kebabs, and they are excellent. Their chips are also first rate, and while the decor is awful, the service patchy and the old Greek men that invariably are sit-

Below: the Burswood Casino.

Left: party people at Rise.

admission charge; train:
Fremantle
Large club with eight bars
and live bands. Another
stayer on the nightlife scene.

The Red Sea
83 Rokeby Road, Subiaco; tel:
08-9382 2022; Thur–Sat
8pm–late; admission charge;
train: Subiaco; map p.132 B3
Popular nightclub with several bars and dance floors.

Rise Dance Club
139 James Street, Northbridge;
tel: 08-9328 7447;
www.rise.net.au; Wed–Sat
8pm–late, Sun 8pm–midnight;
admission charge; train: Perth;
map p.134 A3
The Rise claims 'it's all about
the dancing', and with their
massive central dance floor,
complete with podiums, they
probably mean it. Expect
dance and techno, lots of
lights and loud music.

Above: the distinctive signage
of the Brass Monkey pub.

ting out the front always
surly, this place does well
for both its late hours and
great food.

Fast Eddys
454 Murray Street; tel: 08-9321
2552; daily 24 hours; train:
Perth; map p.133 E3
Fast Eddys is an American
diner-style café, where the
burgers are big and sloppy
but tasty. The fries are
chunky and loaded with salt,
often just what you crave
after a night out. The café
has a large menu, but there is
also a walk-in takeaway area
that does burgers, hot dogs
and chips. An institution.

Oriel Café
483 Hay Street, Subiaco; tel: 08-
9382 1886; daily 24 hours; train:
Subiaco; map p.134 B2
Oriel offers a large menu,
ranging across all tastes and
styles. The food probably
won't change your life, but it's
a decent café, and if you're
hungry for a proper meal, it's
about your best option.

Nightclubs
Metro City
146 Roe Street, Northbridge; tel:
08-9228 0500; www.metro
superclub.com; Thur–Sat
9pm–late, from 8pm for live
music; admission charge; train:
Perth; map p.134 A3
Metro's (as locals call it) is
just about Perth's number-
one club, that is, if you like a
mix of Top 40 R 'n' B, electro
and party music. When it's
not a club, it's a popular
place for visiting bands to
play, plus they often have
international DJs spinning
the decks.

Metropolis Fremantle
58 South Terrace, Fremantle; tel:
08-9336 1880; www.metropolis
fremantle.com.au; Fri–Sat
8pm–late, Sun 8pm–midnight;

Of late, taxis have been an
issue in Perth: there simply
aren't enough where and when
you need them, especially from
midnight onwards on popular
nights. Taxis are also starting
to choose longer fares over
shorter ones, so if you call one
to where you are staying, but
don't want to go far, keep
calling the taxi company to
make sure one is on its way.
Another tip is that taxi drivers
aren't fond of taking inebriated
people home, especially if it's a
large group of men only. So
look responsible, don't act like
a larrikin, and you've got a
better shot at getting home by
wheels rather than foot. Also if
you have an 'accident' in a cab,
you will be charged a hefty
cleaning fee. Taxis accept cash
and most credit cards. Reliable
firms include: **Swan Taxis**
(tel: 13 13 30) and **Black and
White Taxis** (tel: 13 10 08).

Pampering

With Perth's booming economy there seems to be no shortage of ways to spend money. The spa and beauty scene is thriving, with more and more salons and wellness centres offering treatments for men as well as women. The trend in Perth is to treat spa and beauty treatments as seriously as a haircut, an important part of maintenance and overall well-being. However, even though many locals would like to visit day spas frequently, the treatments are not cheap and sometimes get reserved for special occasions, so do call ahead if you feel like treating yourself to some special Perth pampering.

Beauty Products

Kit Cosmetics
200 Murray Street (inside Myer); tel: 08-9265 5872; www.kitcosmetics.com.au; Mon–Sat 9am–6pm, Fri until 9pm, Sun noon–5pm; train: Perth; map p.134 A2
Kit stocks lust-worthy beauty products from around the world and is the younger, funkier sister to Mecca. Both men and women are looked after, and you'll always discover something fun and interesting to play with. Staff are friendly and happy to help.

For a spa experience you won't forget, head to **Hidden Valley Eco Spa**. In Pickering Brook, around 45 minutes from Perth, Hidden Valley offers guests chalet accommodation, a large menu of day spa services, in-room dining, and can even organise special extras such as long-stemmed roses on arrival, or a chauffeured Rolls Royce to take you on a trip to a local winery. www.hiddenvalleyeco.com

Mecca Cosmetica
Claremont Shopping Centre, Bay View Terrace, Claremont; tel: 08-9286 2477; www.mecca cosmetica.com.au; Mon–Sat 9am–5pm, Thur until 8pm; train: Claremont
If you like the best of the best when it comes to skincare and make-up, Mecca Cosmetica is a must. Stocking perfumes, skin care, make-up, toothpaste, nail polish and more for both men and women, you can lose hours poring over the luxurious brands. Staff are well informed on the products; make sure you ask for help, as you will learn much more and be pointed in the right direction. Brands include Nars, Stila, Martin+Goetz, NV Perricone, Philosophy, Kiehl's, Du Wop, Kevyn Aucoin and Bumble and Bumble.

Salons and Spas

Affinity Day Spa
16 Station Street, Cottesloe; tel: 08-9284 4333; www.affinity dayspa.com.au; Mon–Sat 9am–5.30pm, Thur until 9pm, Sat until 5pm; train: Cottesloe

Situated in Cottesloe, one of Perth's most luxurious suburbs, this lush day spa offers a wide range of treatments, from packages of facials and massages lasting hours to acrylic nails, body wraps, oxygen face treatments, hydrotherapy and tanning.

Element Aveda Concept Salon
4/317 Murray Street; tel: 08-9322 8155; Tue–Sat 10am–6pm, Thur until 8pm; train: Perth; map p.134 A2
Using the cult brand Aveda, this salon specialises in beauty treatments, massage, hair and make-up. It is a tranquil space in the city's trendy Wolf Lane, a tiny cobbled lane running off Murray Street.

Guys Grooming
Shop G5, 160 Central Arcade, 811 Hay Street; tel: 08-9226 3022; www.guysgrooming. com.au; Mon–Fri 8am–6pm; train: Perth; map p.134 A2
Offering a place for guys to go that is definitely a male space, with all grooming needs taken care of. Haircuts, traditional face shaves, waxing, massage, facials,

Left: the beauty emporium of Mecca Cosmetica.

fans think he's a genius, so if your brows are bushy, go see him. It's not cheap, but you'll either receive a free eyebrow gel, mini tweezers or a discount off products purchased.

Spa at the Richardson

The Richardson Hotel, 32 Richardson Street; tel: 08-9217 8870; www.therichardson. com.au; daily from 10am, bookings required; bus: red CAT; map p.133 D3

This spa is in the boutique Richardson Hotel *(see Hotels, p.66)*, but you don't have to be a guest to stay here. The spa is Asian-style with dark timbers, soothing music and top treatments including facials, massage and wraps.

manicures and pedicures are all on offer.

Keturah Spa and Skincare

5/500 Beaufort Street, Highgate; tel: 08-9228 0855; www.keturah.com.au; Mon–Sat 9am–5.30pm; bus: 67; map p.134 C4

Keturah was one of the pioneers of the beauty scene in Perth and now has a long list of available services, including a list for men. Beyond the usual array of facials and massages, Keturah also do microdermabrasion, peels, light treatments, water therapy and have an infra-red sauna.

Le Beau Day Spa

75 Gilbertson Road, Kardinya; tel: 08-9331 1122; www.day-spa-perth.com; Mon–Sat 9am–5pm; bus: 940

Le Beau is the most awarded day spa in the Perth area, and while externally the location doesn't appear to be that tranquil, once you are through the doors, the world disappears. There is a Balinese-style relaxation area,

hydrobath, Vichy shower, eight-seater outdoor spa and sauna. Treatments include Indian oil massage, hot stone therapy, waxing, tanning, nails, and facials using Guinot, Gatineau and Thalgo. There is Napoleon Perdis make-up, too. At the end of facials and massages you are given a cleansing fruit platter, juice and left to relax for as long as you like.

Matt Yuko

30/22 St Quentin's Avenue, Claremont; tel: 08-9385 2006; Mon–Sat 9am–5pm; train: Claremont

Matt Yuko specialises in eyebrows. And that's it. His

Right: indulge in some relaxation at one of Perth's day spas.

Parks

There are numerous parks in the city centre where you can while away some time in the almost perennially pleasant weather. However, if you fancy venturing futher afield, there are beautiful national parks located within driving distance of Perth; generally speaking, access to the parks is best by car. When walking in the Western Australian national parks, wear a wide-brimmed hat, sunscreen with a sun protection factor of 30-plus and sturdy shoes. Take plenty of drinking water with you, at least three litres per day, more if the weather is very hot. In most park areas you will not be able to access clean drinking water.

City Parks

Araluen Botanical Gardens

Croyden Road, off Brookton Highway; tel: 08-9496 1171; daily; admission charge; by car

Araluen is one of Perth's greatest attractions. Bush walks by flowing streams and picnic spots among spectacular garden displays are boosted with mass plantings of bulbs, annuals and other plants from August through to October. Araluen is an eastern states Aboriginal word meaning 'singing waters' or 'place of lilies'. A 'Grove of the Unforgotten' is a tribute to 88 Young Australia League members killed in World War I. Araluen was restored by the government in the 1990s, and new works include a spectacular watercourse.

The Esplanade

Bordered by Barrack Street and Riverside Drive; daily; free; bus: blue CAT; map p.134 A1

The Esplanade overlooks Barrack Square and the Swan River and is essentially just a nice open place, without too many plants, but it's

Above: the State War Memorial Cenotaph obelisk in Kings Park.

where you'll find lots of activity over city lunch breaks. Outdoor exercise classes are held here, and during the Perth International Arts Festival (see p.54) it is also the location for the purpose-built Beck's Music Box, where a range of contemporary music is performed.

You'll also notice a pyramid-shaped greenhouse. Called the Allan Green Conservatory, it houses exotic tropical plants and rare palms (Sat–Sun 10am–4pm and public holidays noon–4pm; free). Across the park at Barrack Square are the Swan Bells (see p.6;

www.swanbells.com.au; daily 10am–4.30pm; admission charge); to see the bells being rung, check the times online. You can pay to climb to the top of the bell tower and the view is worth it, plus you get a look inside the interesting glass structure.

Heirisson Island

Near Causeway, end of Riverside Drive; free; train: Perth; map p.139 D3–E4

The walk from Barrack Street Jetty to Heirisson Island can be done comfortably in 30 minutes. At the end of Riverside Drive follow the path up onto the Causeway, turn

Left: native gum trees in Kings Park.

The first public park in the city was Queen's Gardens, in East Perth. It was created in 1899 out of clay pits that for 50 years supplied bricks for buildings such as Perth Town Hall. Lily ponds and English trees show the gardens' British influences, as does the 1927 statue of Peter Pan, a replica of the one that stands in London's Kensington Gardens.

right off the Causeway, and follow the track down towards an orange sign, with the river on your right. A small colony of western grey kangaroos are housed in an enclosure here, bringing an iconic bush element right into the city. During the heat of the day kangaroos stay under cover, but if you move quietly around the track there's a good chance of finding them grazing.

There is a 2km (1-mile) track around Heirisson Island. At the southern tip is a bronze statue of Yagan, an Aboriginal leader killed in 1833. The statue has been vandalised on numerous occasions over the years.

The island was named after a French sailor, midshipman François Heirisson. Long before the founding of Perth, he rowed a longboat all the way upriver to the island from his moored ship *Le Naturaliste*, which carried Nicolas Baudin's scientific expedition of 1801–4. As late as the 1920s, squatters lived rough in shacks on the island, in sight of Govern-

ment House. In 1984 an Aboriginal camp lasted for 40 days before its occupants, land-rights protesters, were evicted. The Aboriginal community has recently allowed outdoor concerts to be held here; up to 30,000 young partygoers convened on the island to hear Kanye West and Cypress Hill in 2008.

Hyde Park

Cnr Vincent, William, Glendower and Throssell streets; Wed–Sat 7am–5pm, Sun 7am–1pm; free; bus: 67; map p.134 B4

Hyde Park is a beautiful space, filled with mature trees. In the centre of the park is a small lake surrounded by weeping willows. There is playground equipment, a water playground, free electric barbecues, drinking fountains and public toilets. It is a meeting point for Aboriginal families, and the path around the lake is well frequented by walkers and joggers. In the surrounding streets you'll discover beautiful examples of 'federation' and terrace homes. On the nearby Lincoln Street there is a Swiss-French bak-

ery called the Pearl of Highgate, ideal for picking up picnic goodies. A secret worth several visits.

Kings Park

Off Kings Park Road; Park Visitor Information tel: 08-9480 3634; www.bgpa.wa.gov.au; daily 9.30am–4pm; park access daily 24 hours; free; bus: 102, 78, 24, 37; map p.132–3 B1–D2, 136–7 A3–D4

Kings Park is integral to Perth's identity. There's no other city in the world with as big an area of natural bushland at its centre. Much of

Below: the monument of Queen Victoria in Kings Park.

the park is rough bushland, with walking paths running throughout. There are beautiful cultivated lawns, terraces and water gardens throughout the park, many positioned to take in sweeping views of the Swan River, thanks to the park's high vantage point over the city and river. The park covers 400 hectares (988 acres), and Park Visitor Information offers free half-day bush and wildflower walks conducted by volunteer guides.

The park is full of war memorials, and Fraser Avenue is no exception. The ranks of magnificent lemon-scented gums, known as the widow-maker's tree on account of its habit of shedding large branches during times of drought, were planted to mark WA's 1929 centenary. Individual gums lining May Avenue and Lovekin Drive commemorate the fallen of two world wars. As well as the Cenotaph, other memorials commemorate victims of the Bali bombing of 2002, Western Australian victims of the South African War of 1899–1902 (just off Fraser Avenue) and victims of the Vietnam War (near Western Power playground).

A memorial to the Australians who fought and died on the Kokoda Trail during the Japanese invasion of Papua New Guinea in World War II is also found nearby. If you stay on the road, rather than the path, you will approach the Cenotaph through the Whispering Wall, which commemorates battles in which Australians have fought. The huge river gum just past here was planted by Elizabeth II in 1954, during one of her Australian tours.

Beyond the Cenotaph are the heavily planted sections of the **Botanic Gardens** (daily 24 hours; free). Any of the paths to the right will lead to exotic plants and trees, including many hundreds of native species.

By keeping to the left-hand path, with the Swan River on your left, you will come to a Tree-Top Walk with views across the river, and then enter an area of native bush (stay on the marked paths), eventually exiting the park on Park Avenue, in an exclusive neighbourhood called Crawley, located about 2km (1 mile) west from the University of Western Australia (see below right). Back in the Botanic Gardens, between the riverside path and Forest Drive, is the Pioneer Women's Memorial, a grassy bowl with an ornamental lake and fountain that doubles as an open-air venue in summer.

Close by is the Broadwalk, a grassy swath with a high lookout, known as the DNA tower because of its twin circular staircases; from here you can see Rottnest Island (see p.46–8) about 30km (18 miles) away. The Broadwalk leads, after about 2km (1½ miles), to the Western Power children's playground and lake. Lycopod Island in the centre of the lake has model dinosaurs and timber-and-steel lycopods (the world's first trees), and calamites (fern-like plants). In the lake, replicas of 3.5-billion-year-old stromatolites are inset

Left: contemplation at the State War Memorial Cenotaph, on the edge of Kings Park.

Above: the towers of the CBD loom over Stirling Gardens.

with solar cells to power the misty spray.

In a steel cage near the lake is a growing 'dinosaur tree', a Wollemi Pine, thought to have been extinct until recently. In the 1990s a grove of such trees was discovered in a secret gorge in Wollemi National Park, New South Wales. Rare examples were sent to important botanical authorities, and soon the propagation and sale of the pines was well under way.

Stirling Gardens
Cnr St Georges Terrace and Barrack Street; daily; free; bus: blue CAT; map p.134 B1

Below: Government House, in Stirling Gardens.

Stirling Gardens, named after Captain James Stirling, who founded Perth, are the oldest gardens in the city. They were started in the 1830s and in 1845 opened as a botanical garden. In 1960, Kings Park Botanic Garden opened, ending the need for Stirling Gardens to be the state's botanic park. At the entrance of the gardens is a statue of Alexander Forrest who was an explorer and early mayor of Perth. Within the gardens you'll also find kangaroo sculptures, a water feature and sculptures of Snugglepot and Cuddlepie, characters from May Gibbs's children's book of the same name. The gardens border Council House, where the Perth Lord Mayor's offices are situated.

Supreme Court Gardens
Cnr Barrack Street and River-side Drive; daily; free; bus: blue CAT; map p.134 A1–B1

The Supreme Court Gardens (*see p.8*) merge with Stirling Gardens and are a beautiful, quiet place to while away a break in the city. During the summer, large outdoor con-certs are held here, with up to 8,000 people converging on the garden space. At

Christmas, this is the location for Carols by Candlelight. There is a large central grassed area fringed with tropical-looking verdant plants, with some park benches on the periphery if you don't feel like lying on the lawn. Across Barrack Street you will find the Esplanade.

University of Western Australia
Winthrop Avenue, Subiaco; daily; free; bus: 78, 102; map p.136 A2

UWA was the first free university of the British Commonwealth. Across the Reflecting Pool is Winthrop Hall, with its undercroft terracotta frieze of gryphons and 50m (164ft) clock tower. To the right across Whitfield Court, the colonnaded building is the original library (now admin), and more pillars hold up Hackett Hall, on the left. All were built in 1932 with an endowment from Sir John Winthrop Hackett, the first Chancellor of UWA and also the owner of Perth's daily news-paper, *The West Australian*. The design was by the Victorian architects Sayce and Alsop, who won an international competition for the commission.

The grounds of the University of Western Australia are worth taking an amble around. Stop in at the visitor centre (north end of the admin building) near Winthrop Hall off Winthrop Avenue and ask to be shown where the prettiest areas are: they have booklets and often guided tours are run. The sunken garden is a popular spot to get married in, but there are other places worth a visit, too. Peacocks stroll around the Greek-Revival-style architecture, too.

National Parks

Cape Range
Admission charge; by car

Lying predominantly on the western side of Northwest Cape Peninsula, Cape Range National Park protects an area of 50,581 hectares (126,453 acres). The northern boundary of the park is 39km (24 miles) from Exmouth by road, and the southern boundary is 70km (43 miles) north of Coral Bay.

The time to visit is between April and September, when you'll have the best weather to go for walks, see wildlife, picnic, camp, canoe and explore caves. Nearby Ningaloo Marine Park

offers some of the world's best dives, and in season you can dive with majestic whale sharks.

There are a number of camping areas all along the stunning, white sandy coast, from Boat Harbour to Ned's Camp. Entry fees apply. There are also picnic facilities and toilets at many sites. No campfires are allowed in the park: gas barbecues only.

The Cape Range is the only elevated limestone range on the northwestern coast of WA. The impressive weathered limestone range has plateaus of up to 314m (1,030ft) high. It forms the spine of the peninsula that stretches up towards Northwest Cape in the Gascoyne region of Western Australia. You can climb up deep rocky gorges to enjoy breathtaking scenery. One of many popular walks is a 3km (2-mile) ramble through Mandu Mandu Gorge along the bed of an ancient river. As the summer heat is intense, walks should only be attempted between April and September. You can also view rock wallabies at Yardie Creek.

Beneath the rocky plateaux and canyons of the

Cape Range National Park lies a network of hidden caves and tunnels. They harbour a unique collection of bizarre cave-dwelling animals: an ancient treasure trove of immense value to both science and nature conservation.

D'Entrecasteaux
Admission charge; by car

The D'Entrecasteaux National Park stretches along the coast for 130km (81 miles) from Black Point (35km/22 miles east of Augusta), to Long Point (10km/6 miles west of Walpole) and extends inland for between 5 and 20km (3–12 miles). It lies 8km (5 miles) from Northcliffe and 40km (25 miles) from Pemberton.

Spectacular coastal cliffs, beaches, mobile sand dunes, vast coastal wildflower heaths and even pockets of karri are all part of the scenery of D'Entrecasteaux National Park. The park has isolated beach campsites, wild coastal vistas and excellent fishing. Much of the park is managed for its wilderness values, so few facilities are provided.

Major streams and rivers, including the Warren, Donnelly and Shannon, drain through D'Entrecasteaux and empty into its coastal waters. High sand dunes and limestone cliffs on the sea coast give way to coastal heathlands and a series of lakes and swamps further inland. These include Lake Yeagarup and Lake Jasper, which is the largest freshwater lake in the southern half of Western Australia. Vast areas of wetlands behind the coastal dunes are known as The Blackwater. Another outstanding feature is the Yeagarup Dune, an impressive mobile dune 10km (6 miles) long.

Below: typical Western Austrailian bush terrain.

Above: watch out for emus and kangaroos in the bush: both are fairly common sights.

Much of the park is off limits to cars, especially if you don't have a four-wheel-drive. The basalt columns west of Black Point are one of the park's most stunning landforms. This feature originated from a volcanic lava flow some 135 million years ago. The formation resulted from the slow cooling of a deep pool of lava, similar to the development of mud cracks. In the process of it cracking and shrinking, columns were formed perpendicular to the surface. The result was a close-packed series of hexagonal columns, now slowly being eroded by the sea.

There are several beaches suitable for car access: Windy Harbour, Salmon Beach and Broke Inlet are the only coastal areas of this large park which are accessible by conventional vehicle. Four-wheel-drive tracks lead to other coastal fishing and camping spots. Stay on existing tracks and reduce your tyre pressure in summer to cope with sand. Sand tracks make travelling slow inside the park. Many places, such as the mouth of the

Donnelly River, can be reached only by small boat. Significant vehicle-exclusion areas provide those who are willing to hike with an opportunity to experience seclusion on a deserted beach. If you intend to go walking, make sure you are properly equipped with map, compass, water and sun protection, as this is wild country. There are campsites throughout the park, some with small camping fees.

John Forrest National Park
Free; by car

John Forrest is one of Australia's oldest conservation areas and Western Australia's first national park. The area was first established in 1898 as a reserve to conserve its many natural and cultural features.

It became John Forrest National Park in 1947, in honour of the famous WA explorer and statesman. Recreation is an important use of John Forrest National Park. It provides magnificent vistas of the Swan coastal plain and contains walk trails through rugged wilderness, along the old railway line or

to quiet pools and spectacular waterfalls.

On the western boundary of the park is the Rocky Pool picnic area, which is set among attractive wandoo and paperbark woodland. Here, after winter rains, you can sit and watch the waters

---

When driving on country roads, be aware that kangaroos can jump in front of your car, and emus can run onto the road. These animals are most active at dawn and dusk, so take extra care at these times. Kangaroos especially can become stunned by car headlights. If a roo does jump in front of your car, do not attempt to swerve and miss it. The best thing to do is to keep going following the direction of the road, as swerving means you could hit a tree at the side of the road, and probably also still hit a roo. They often travel in groups, so if you see one, there's probably another close behind. If it seems like a kangaroo might hit your car and come through the windscreen, put your arms up across your face so their scratching claws don't get your face and chest.

93

of Jane Brook tumble down a series of small rapids into the pool.

In summer the hills area can get very hot, so the best time to visit is in autumn, winter and spring, when you can enjoy a relaxing picnic or bush stroll.

Leeuwin-Naturaliste
Free; by car

Leeuwin-Naturaliste National Park stretches 120km (75 miles) from Bunker Bay in the north to Augusta in the south. Most roads in the area are sealed. Gravel roads are usually suitable for two-wheel-drive vehicles.

Between Cowaramup Bay and Karridale, the Leeuwin-Naturaliste Park features some of its most rugged and inaccessible coastline. Facing due west, the coastal cliffs and rocky shoreline bear the brunt of giant ocean swells generated across thousands of miles of ocean by the prevailing westerly and southwesterly winds.

Punctuated along the coast are scenic lookouts from which to marvel at the ocean's beauty and power.

You might be lucky enough to see humpback and southern right whales from various vantage points along the coast, and bush-walking attracts people right into the heart of the park.

There are several short walks and trails through this area, and the beach scenery is spectacular. The Cape to Cape Walk track runs 140km (87 miles) from Cape Naturaliste to Cape Leeuwin, but you can break it down into smaller sections. Brochures are available on walktrails at Cape Naturaliste, Yallingup, Margaret River and the Cape to Cape Walk. There are several camping areas with some basic facilities.

Right: a stretch of Leeuwin-Naturaliste National Park's coastline.

Yalgorup
Free; by car

Yalgorup National Park lies on the western edge of the Swan Coastal Plain just south of the new Dawesville Channel near Mandurah.

The name Yalgorup is derived from two Noongar Aboriginal words: *Yalgor*, meaning a swamp or lake, and *up*, a suffix meaning a place. In the early 1970s Yalgorup National Park was formally established to protect the coastal lakes, swamps and tuart woodland between Mandurah and Myalup Beach. The park is of significant scientific interest: the dune systems are a result of changes in sea level changing hundreds of thousands of years ago, right up to the end of the last Ice Age around 10,000 years ago. The lakes in the park are surrounded with important waterbird habitat, but more interestingly, rock-like structures

Above: a koala dozes in Yanchep National Park.

called thrombalites can be found on the edge of Lake Clifton. While they look like rocks, thrombalites are alive, built by micro-organisms. These organisms were the only known form of life on Earth from 3,500 million to 650 million years ago.

Today, living examples of these once completely dominant organisms are restricted to only a few places. So why do thrombolites grow at Yalgorup? Scientists have suggested it is perhaps because Lake Clifton is associated with upwellings of fresh groundwater that are high in calcium carbonate. The micro-organisms living in this shallow lake environment are able to precipitate calcium carbonate from the waters as they photosynthesise, forming the mineralised structure that is the thrombolite.

The significance of thrombolites and stromatolites to science is inestimable, but they are very fragile and can be degraded by visitors walking over them. To protect the thrombolites, an observation walkway has been built to minimise any impact from visitors wanting to see these fascinating structures.

Yanchep National Park
Free; by car

Only 51km (32 miles) north of Perth, reaching this park will only require a 45-minute drive. Just follow Wanneroo Road north about 25km (16 miles) past Wanneroo and you will see the Yanchep National Park signs. Known as Perth's natural and cultural meeting place, Yanchep National Park is home to many native birds and lots of kangaroos.

The National Park environment provides a unique setting to experience environmental and cultural activities that are informative and promote awareness about our natural areas. Several of the caves in Yanchep National Park have been open for tourists during the past 70 years. These include Cabaret, Mambibby, Yanchep, Yonderup and Crystal caves. There have been more than 600 caves documented in the park.

There are self-guided walks, plus a boardwalk that has been built in order for visitors to enjoy the koalas that live in the park.

Pubs and Bars

As in the rest of the country, going to the pub is a popular pastime of West Australians, and many establishments offer good menus alongside the beer. Legislation changes in Perth in 2008 meant that smaller bars seating up to 80 people could come more easily into existence, with the hope that Perth would develop more of the quirky, small-bar culture that Melbourne has, and less of the barn-style pubs that have existed for so long. While this legislation has yet to make a profound difference, the European style of wine bar offering a small tapas-style menu is increasingly popular with punters.

Swan River and Kings Park

Amphoras
1303 Hay Street; tel: 08-9226 4666; Tue–Sat, daily 7am–late; bus: red CAT; map p.133 D3
This new bar offers a good wine list which errs on the fancier, pricier side, and a concise but solid tapas menu. Packed out on Friday nights, it has a great vibe.

The Lucky Shag Waterfront Bar
Barrack Street Jetty; tel: 08-9221 6011; daily 11am–late; bus: blue CAT; map p.134 A1
This popular pub overlooks the river, with a good range of beers and wines, plus live music and DJs at weekends. Food is available, too. In case

you're wondering, shags are seabirds and they are often seen perched by the water drying their wings.

City Centre

Belgian Beer Café
Westende, Cnr King and Murray streets; tel: 9321 4094; daily 11am–midnight, Sun until 10pm; train: Perth; map p.134 A2
This unique pub serves modern Belgian fare, including mussels, venison sausage and mouthwatering Belgian waffles. There is plenty of outdoor seating on the street or in the garden at the rear, where you can enjoy one of the beers on tap, including Hoegaarden,

Leffe and Kriek. Great for dining, or you may like to join the Friday night throng of exuberant city workers for a drink. A cone of frites with aioli is a must.

Leederville

Fibber McGee's
711 Newcastle Street; tel: 08-9227 0800; daily 11am–midnight, Sun until 10pm; map p.133 E4
Not far from the busy Oxford Street intersection, Fibber McGee's is an Irish pub with a good range of beers plus a menu big on comfort food. For example, the steak-and-stout pie comes out looking like a pastry-topped football. All portions are on the very large side.

Leederville Hotel
742 Newcastle Street; tel: 08-9286 0150; daily 11am–

> Where bars are said to stay open 'late', that means between 2 and 4am (although sometimes they will remain open until 6am in the summer).

Left: the Lucky Shag.

Left: a trip to the bar at The Brass Monkey.

ley; tel: 08-9328 6200; daily 11am–midnight, Fri–Sat until 1am, Sun until 10pm; bus: 67, 21
An English-style pub serving top-notch burgers and pizzas. Its Thursday karaoke has a cult following. Check out the model train set that runs above the bar.

Grapeskin

209 William Street; tel: 08-9227 9596; daily 11am–late; train: Perth; map p.134 A3
Part of The Brass Monkey, but operates as a separate restaurant. At weekends it buzzes with people dropping in to buy wine from the cellar, others chatting over drinks at the front bar or enjoying dinner at the rear.

Luxe Bar

446 Beaufort Street, Highgate; tel: 08-9228 9680; Wed–Sun 7pm–late; bus: blue CAT; map p.134 C4
Luxe has mastered the art of cocktail couture and employs bartenders that have won awards for their craft. Plush, glamorous interior, gay- and straight-friendly.

Below: a cheeky sign at the Belgian Beer Café.

midnight, Sun until 10pm; train: Leederville
The big nights at the Leederville are Wednesdays and Sundays, when a young crowd packs out the beer garden in summer and the indoor dance floor in winter. It caters to many moods: simply sit and have a quiet drink with a friend, enjoy a game of pool or get up and boogie.

Niche Bar

Off Oxford Street (city end); tel: 08-9227 1007; www.niche bar.com; Wed, Fri, Sat 7pm–late; train: Leederville
You'll find this hip bar by walking through the car park at the end of Oxford Street, which is close to the railway station and freeway. Think 1970s style: white shag-pile and lots of couches.

East Perth

The Royal Bar on the Waterfront

60 Royal Street; tel: 08-9221 0466; www.theroyaleast perth.com; daily 11am–late; bus: red CAT; map p.135 D2
The Royal occupies enviable waterfront real estate in East Perth. Serving a range of

beers on tap, including WA's own Colonial Brewing, The Royal has recently come under new ownership.

Northbridge

The Brass Monkey

209 William Street, Cnr James Street; tel: 08-9227 9596; daily 11am–late; train: Perth; map p.134 A3
The Brass Monkey is a Perth landmark and institution. Several different bar areas and plenty of Australian beers on offer, including many of Matilda Bay's beers on tap.

The Brisbane Hotel

292 Beaufort Street, Highgate; tel: 08-9227 2300; Mon–Tue 11.30am–late, Wed–Sat 11am–midnight, Sun until 10pm; bus: blue CAT; map p.134 B4
Possibly the most stylish hotel in Perth, the Brisbane is relaxed and funky. You can pop in for a drink, but the food is worth staying for, so grab a table in the shady garden. From a table you can get waiter service if you pop your credit card behind the bar.

The Flying Scotsman

639 Beaufort Street, Mount Law-

Above: mojito at Llama Bar.

The Queens
520 Beaufort Street, Highgate; tel: 08-9328 7267; Mon–Fri 11am–midnight, Sat 7am–midnight, Sun 7am–10pm; bus: 67, 21

Boasting a huge, leafy outdoor area, the Queens is a great spot for a cold beer on a sunny day. Inside the building is all about floorboards and rustic brick walls. Sample some of WA's best beer on tap here, from Matilda Bay Brewery.

Universal Bar
221 William Street; tel: 08-9227 6771; Wed–Sat 11am–2am, Sun until 10pm; train: Perth; map p.134 A3

Universal gets in some great jazz and blues bands. A new upstairs terrace bar is open at the rear. The small upstairs ara features a small section that opens up to the night sky in good weather.
SEE ALSO MUSIC AND DANCE, P.81

Subiaco

Llama Bar
1/464 Hay Street; tel: 08-9388 0222; Tue–Sat 5pm–late; train: Subiaco; map p.134 B2

With a cocktail list as long as your arm and a small list of nibbles, you can be guaranteed a late night. The entrance is on Rokeby Road.

The Subiaco Hotel
Cnr Hay and Rokeby streets; tel: 08-9381 3069; www.subiaco hotel.com.au; daily 7am–late; train: Subiaco; map p.132 B3

This pub has a couple of distinct drinking areas: a sports bar on one side and on the other, a designated chill area, with low-slung seats and couches. There is also a restaurant as part of the elegant building and the food is excellent. Popular on Fridays and after football games.
SEE ALSO RESTAURANTS, P.106

The Vic
226 Hay Street; tel: 08-6380 8222; daily 11am–midnight, Sun until 10pm; train: Subiaco; map p.132 C3

This pub serves excellent pub grub, and its outdoor garden is divine in good weather. There are daily specials, and good lunch deals such as beer-battered fish and chips and a middy of Redback (a medium-sized glass of a local wheat beer) for just A$12. Other dishes such as teriyaki beef stir-fry, steak sandwiches and pasta dishes are always reliable. The bar packs out on a Friday night and whenever there's a game on at the nearby Subiaco Oval.

Fremantle

Little Creatures
40 Mews Road; tel: 08-9430 5155; Mon–Fri 10am–midnight, Sat–Sun 9am–midnight; train: Fremantle

Once a crocodile farm, this huge shed now houses one of Perth's best breweries. Serving its own beer and a range of wine, its semi-industrial yet welcoming interior draws huge crowds. The food is good, too: try the frites with aioli, the mussels or any of the pizzas.

Several of Perth's big pubs are owned by the one group, ALH, so you will notice similarities between them, especially in the range of beers on tap. Some in the group include The Queens, The Vic and The Sail and Anchor.

A favourite hangout of Fremantle's young and funky set.

The Norfolk
47 South Terrace; tel: 08-9335 5405; Mon–Sat 11am–midnight, Sun 8.30am–10pm; train: Fremantle

The Norfolk's limestone-walled courtyard is a wonderful spot to while away a warm afternoon. The leafy outdoor area is often busy, but you'll find more room inside. The food is good-quality pub grub, ranging from light seafood to more substantial fare.

The Sail and Anchor
64 South Terrace; tel: 08-9335 8433; Mon–Thur 11am–midnight, Fri–Sat until 1am, Sun until 10pm; train: Fremantle

This was the first microbrewery in Perth. Still producing great beers, it has recently had a face-lift and now has a funky courtyard to complement the grand building. The upstairs area has a chilled bar feel, while downstairs the atmosphere is like that of a traditional pub. The menu includes a wide range of tapas as well as more substantial mains.

Cottesloe, Claremont, Swanbourne and Scarborough

The Claremont
Cnr Bay View Terrace, Claremont; tel: 08-9286 0123; www.the claremont.com.au; Mon–Wed noon–midnight, Thur–Sat until 1am, Sun until 10pm; train: Claremont

The Claremont is a stalwart

of the western suburbs' scene. Thursday is its biggest night, but you'll find people here almost any time of day. The building is an old-style terrace, and punters sit outside on elevated boards just above street level.

Cottesloe Beach Hotel
104 Marine Parade, Cottesloe; tel: 08-9383 1100; www. cottesloebeachhotel.com.au; daily 11am–midnight, Sun until 10pm; train: Cottesloe, bus: 102
The Cott, as it's known to locals, is packed out on any fair-weather day. On Sunday afternoons the front terrace area packs out as people try to get a prime sunset-watching position, but there is a huge beer garden out the back, too. A young, lively crowd. The hotel also offers a free shuttle service between the pub and Cottesloe train station during summer from 3pm to 11pm.

Ocean Beach Hotel
Marine Parade, Cottesloe; tel: 08-9383 5402; daily 11am–midnight, Sun until 10pm; train: Cottesloe, bus: 102
The OBH is a must-go for anyone wanting to experience a true piece of Australian pub culture. You'll fight to get space on a warm afternoon as customers jos-

tle to secure a prime location at the front of the bar, the place to be to watch the sun set over the ocean. A standard range of drinks is on offer.

Stamford Arms
The Esplanade, Scarborough; tel: 08-9340 5771; Mon–Sat 10am–midnight, Sun 10am–10pm; bus: 400
The Stamford Arms is a magnet for a young, boisterous crowd. Near the beach, it is the centre of all action at Scarborough. The pub itself is English-style and has a good range of UK beers.

Swan Valley and the Perth Hills

Duckstein Brewery
9720 West Swan Road, Henley Brook; tel: 08-9296 0620; Wed–Thur 11am–9pm, Fri–Sat until 11pm, Sun until 7pm; by car
This German brewery not only makes excellent beer, but has a huge list of German food to accompany it. The Brewer's Pan, a fry packed with pan-fried potatoes, kassler smoked pork cutlets and bratwurst sausages, is recommended.

Elmar's in the Valley
8731 West Swan Road, Henley Brook; tel: 08-9296 6354; Wed–Sun 10am–late; by car

Elmar and wife Annette have created their own microbrewery and restaurant serving great German food. Every dish is prepared with care, from the pumpernickel bread to the schweinebraten (German-style roast pork), schnitzels and zweibel (onion) sauce.

The Kalamunda Hotel
43 Railway Road, Kalamunda; tel: 08-9257 1084; Mon–Fri noon–3pm, 6–9pm, Sat–Sun noon–9pm; by car
The Kalamunda Hotel is an elegant building with some good food to match. The menu features old favourites, including a beef-and-Guinness pie made from a secret family recipe. Beers on offer are your standard fare, with several UK beers on tap.

Mash Brewing
10250 West Swan Road, Henley Brook; tel: 08-9296 5588; www.mashbrewing.com.au; Mon–Tue 11am–5pm, Wed–Sat until 9pm, Sun until 8pm; by car
Mash brews seven beers on site – a pale ale, Mexican lager, dark lager, pilsner, wheat beer and one other beer which changes seasonally. There is also a brasserie at the brewery which serves good, tasty food.

Below: Little Creatures in Fremantle.

Restaurants

It has been said that Perth has more cafés and restaurants per capita than anywhere else in Australia. Whether that's true or not, there are a considerable amount of great places to go and sate your hunger for something special. From adventurous Asian to classic Italian, Perth's multicultural bent has certainly paid off when it comes to dining. The city's proximity to the ocean makes seafood a natural highlight, as well as ensures that there are some eateries positioned in stunning locations looking over the water. For further listings of establishments serving good food, see *Cafés, p.32–5*, and *Pubs and Bars, p.96–9*.

Swan River and Kings Park

EAST ASIAN

Shun Fung on the River
6 Barrack Square at Barrack Street Jetty; tel: 08-9221 1868; daily noon–10pm; $$$; bus: blue CAT; map p.134 A1
Top-notch Chinese cuisine is served at this well-located restaurant with views over the Swan River. Some of the more unusual dishes include whole grouper, shark fin and bamboo fungus soup and crispy king prawns with spiced salt and

chilli. There is an emphasis on seafood, with live lobsters and mud crabs kept in tanks. They also do banquet menus for large groups.

EUROPEAN

Zafferano
173 Mounts Bay Road, Crawley; tel: 08-9321 2588; daily noon–11pm, Sat 6–11pm; $$$$; bus: 102, 103, 24; map p.137 D4
Located in the historic Swan Brewery complex, this high-end restaurant boasts some of the prettiest views of the city at night. The menu offers classic Italian seafood dishes, including melt-in-your-mouth crayfish and seafood risotto. The atmosphere and service are upmarket, so it's perfect for a special dinner. Ask for a table with a view.

MODERN AUSTRALIAN

Balthazar
6 The Esplanade; tel: 08-9421 1206; Mon–Fri noon–11pm, Sat–Sun 6–11pm; $$$; train: Perth; map p.134 A2
You won't find Balthazar just

Left: a glass of wine and a light bite at Fraser's Restaurant.

by walking past, but it's worth the effort to look for it. Conveniently located in the CBD on the corner of Howard Street and only a short stroll across the grass from the Swan Bell Tower, this dark, sophisticated restaurant serves some of the best food in town. Known for its massive and interesting wine list, the waiters are very knowledgeable and are happy to advise. Perfect for the indecisive are the tasting plates, which change daily (they even have a dessert tasting plate). Balthazar is a must for foodies, and it is best to book.

Fraser's Restaurant
Fraser Avenue; tel: 08-9481 7100; daily 7am–10pm; $$$; bus: 102, 78, 24, 37; map p.133 D1
Executive Chef Chris Taylor is a proud advocate of top-quality Western Australian produce, and you'll find plenty of it at Fraser's. Expect a varied menu, from dishes such as roast kangaroo loin with potato and celeriac crumble, beetroot and caramelised onion, to char-grilled WA rock lobster with

Left: fine dining at Halo.

menus come with miso soup, lettuce leaves, bean shoots, kimchi, sauces, rice and meat. Bookings are recommended at weekends. BYO.

INDIAN
Nine Mary's
Cnr Hay and Milligan streets; tel: 08-9226 4999; Mon–Fri noon–3pm, 5.30–10.30pm, Sat 5.30–10.30pm; $$; train: Perth; map p.133 E2

Light and bright restaurant serving traditional Indian cuisine. An extensive menu includes good tandoori, alongside a range of curries from mild butter chicken to the fragrant (lamb saag) and the hot (pork vindaloo). Try the mixed tasting plate for starters.

MODERN AUSTRALIAN
C Restaurant Lounge
St Martin's Tower, level 33, 44 St Georges Terrace; tel: 08-9220 8333; Sun–Fri noon–4pm, 6pm–late, Sat 6pm–late; $$$; train: Perth; map p.134 A2

It's worth going to C Restaurant just for the view. Located on the 33rd storey of one of the city's office buildings, this revolving restaurant offers diners a 360° degree view of

Approximate cost of main meal with a glass of wine:	
$$$$	A$50 plus
$$$	A$40–50
$$	A$20–35
$	less than A$20

spicy tomato sauce. The restaurant is situated high up in Kings Park, overlooking the city and the Swan River. You can also just pop in for a morning coffee.

Halo
2 Barrack Square at Barrack Street Jetty; tel: 08-9325 4575; Mon–Fri noon–10pm, Sat–Sun 7am–10pm; $$$; bus: blue CAT; map p.134 A1

Located at the Barrack Street Jetty, with great views of the river (ask for a table with a river view). This is a fine-dining restaurant without any pretension, with most mains coming in around A$30. Where possible, free-range and organic products are used. You'll often find rib-eye steak and scallop stacks on the menu, as well as native foods such as emu and kangaroo.

Matilda Bay Restaurant
3 Hackett Drive, Crawley; tel: 08-9423 5000; Mon–Sat noon–10pm, Sun 7am–10pm; $$$; bus: 102, 103, 24; map p.136 A1

Situated on the banks of the Swan River at Matilda Bay, this restaurant is popular for its beautiful views and peaceful location, making it a good option for a special occasion at reasonable cost. The dinner menu has regular rotisserie items (including kangaroo, fish and duck), fresh crayfish from the tank, plus favourites such as chargrilled sirloin and rack of lamb.

City Centre

EAST ASIAN
Arirang Korean BBQ
91–93 Barrack Street; tel: 08-9225 4855; daily noon–10pm; $$; train: Perth; map p.134 A2

This traditional-style Korean barbecue restaurant is a favourite of locals. Hot coals are loaded under the barbecue plate at your table and you simply cook your choice of meat yourself, creating little lettuce, rice, meat and sauce packages which you eat with your hands. The set

In better restaurants in Perth, BYO ('bring your own' alcohol) is not permitted. Occasionally BYO wine is accepted, but there is often a stiff corkage fee to deter people from doing this. However, there are some gems where they don't mind if you bring your own wine and the corkage is often very reasonable, so definitely ask when you call to book, and ask what the corkage charges are (even though most bottles of wine in Australia now use a stelvin (screw-cap) seal, so technically there is no actual cork to deal with).

Above: a fabulous view from the C Restaurant Lounge.

Perth, from Rottnest Island to Fremantle and across to the Perth Hills. Even if you don't have a full meal here, reserve a table near the window in the bar area and enjoy a couple of first-rate cocktails while watching the sun set.

No. 44 King Street
44 King Street; tel: 9321 4476; daily 6am–11pm; $$–$$$; train: Perth; map p.134 A2

With a menu that changes daily, this is a Perth eating institution where you'll find businesspeople sealing deals over breakfast, locals popping in for a coffee and couples dining at night for a special occasion. The lofty, semi-industrial space allows you to watch baristas, chefs and bakers at work, or you can simply gaze out onto the city's most fashionable street and people-watch. The food is innovative, and there is a large and interesting wine list.

Leederville

EUROPEAN
Duende
662 Newcastle Street; tel: 08-9228 0123; Mon–Sat 6pm–midnight; $$$; train: Leederville

This surprising nook of a restaurant ticks lots of boxes. Atmosphere? Definitely. Top-notch food? Certainly. Amazing wine list? Of course.

Duende is a little slice of Europe, serving fabulous tapas, cheese and other tit-bits in an elegant yet funky setting. Ask for some help with the wine list and perhaps even let the waiter choose for you. It is the sort of place to enjoy a long leisurely evening with lots of tapas and divine wine, and good conversation with friends.

FISH
Kailis Fish Market and Cafe
101 Oxford Street; tel: 08-9443 6300; Mon–Fri 11am–9pm, Sat–Sun 7am–9pm; $$; train: Leederville

On one side of the store is a counter selling some of the best fresh seafood in WA, and on the other side is a seafood restaurant. The Kailis family is one of the biggest local players in seafood, and you will be guaranteed excellent quality, whether it's a fried snapper fillet or fresh tuna sashimi. They also serve great breakfasts. There is another

branch in Fremantle *(see p.35)*, but the dining is far more casual.
SEE ALSO FOOD AND DRINK, P.60

INDIAN
Cinnamon Club
228 Carr Place; tel: 08-9228 1300; Wed–Fri noon–3pm, 5.30–10.30pm, Sat–Tue 5.30–10.30pm; $$; train: Leederville

Traditional Indian cuisine in a funky setting. The mixed tasting plate for starters is generous between two: sample dishes include lamb saag or the goat curry. Salmon fillets from the tandoor oven are moist and generous, and great with mint yoghurt. The traditional Indian desserts are good, too.

SOUTHEAST ASIAN
Ria
106 Oxford Street; tel: 08-9328 2998; Tue–Sat 6–10pm; $$; train: Leederville

If you have any interest in Malaysian food, put Ria on your list of places to visit. From salty chunks of fish served on banana leaves to Mother's moist, caramelised duck, you'll find it difficult to choose just a few dishes. The atmosphere is modern. Be sure to book.

East Perth

MODERN AUSTRALIAN
Cream
Suite 2, 11 Regal Place; tel: 08-9221 0404; Tue–Sat 6pm–late, Friday lunch by reservation; $$$; bus: red CAT; map p.135 D2

Cream is cosy, intimate, relaxed and sophisticated, all at the same time. Chef-owner John Mead is passionate about creating food that is unpretentious, yet top-quality. Everything from pasta to sauces is freshly made in the kitchen, with the exception of the New Norcia bread.

Approximate cost of main meal with a glass of wine:	
$$$$	A$50 plus
$$$	A$40–$50
$$	A$20–35
$	less than A$20

Specialities include crispy-skinned Tasmanian salmon with spicy potato and eggplant salad, and passion fruit soufflé with Belgian white chocolate sorbet.

Friends Restaurant

Hyatt Regency, 20 Terrace Road; tel: 08-9221 0885; Mon–Fri noon–3pm, 6pm–late, Sat–Sun 6pm–late; $$$$; bus: 39, 106, 177; map p.135 C1

This is undeniably one of Perth's poshest restaurants, featuring a massive wine list of aged, rare and simply stunning wines. Many of them are stored in a purpose-built cellar off site simply because they have too many to keep here. The food is similarly extravagant – pheasant layered with foie gras and braised cabbage, wrapped in pastry with celeriac purée and jus; wagyu beef, mushroom ragout, gnocchi, buttered sage, broad beans with a Shiraz and thyme jus. There is also a tasting menu, including wine.

Gershwin's

Hyatt Regency, 99 Adelaide Terrace; tel: 08-9225 1274; Fri–Sat 6.30pm–late; $$$; bus: 39, 106, 177; map p.135 C1

Another excellent option in the Hyatt Regency, this award-winning restaurant has the feel of a New York apartment from the 1920s, with cocktail bar, lounge, three dining areas and a grand

piano. The food is seriously good and visually impressive, and the menu includes many gastronomic delicacies. These are often served in surprising combinations, such as freshwater crayfish bisque and ceviche of scallops and confit salmon.

Lamont's East Perth

11 Brown Street; tel: 08-9202 1566; www.lamonts.com.au; Wed–Sun noon–3pm, 6pm–late; $$$; train: Claisebrook; map p.135 D3

Kate Lamont is one of Perth's best-loved foodies, and her riverside East Perth property is a mecca for those devoted to the plate. Serving freshly prepared and tasty dishes showcasing the best in local produce, Kate has a devoted local following. It is a lovely spot for a leisurely breakfast, too. You can watch families cycle through the parks and boats cruise past on the river while you eat.

SOUTHEAST ASIAN

Basil Leaves

82 Royal Street; tel: 08-9221 8999; Mon–Fri 11.30am–2.30pm, 5pm–late, Sat–Sun 5pm–late; $$; bus: red CAT; map p.135 D2

Serves excellent and beautifully presented Asian cuisine, with an emphasis on Thai and Vietnamese dishes. Lots of the dishes have big fresh flavours which go well with a cold beer

on a hot day. For the cooler months of the year, there are plenty of phad dishes and soups. The staff are very friendly, and the atmosphere is modern and welcoming.

Joe's Oriental Diner

Hyatt Regency, 99 Adelaide Terrace; tel: 08-9225 1268; Mon–Fri noon–2.30pm, 6–10pm, Sat 6–10pm; $$; bus:

> Tipping is not the norm in Western Australia, so don't feel you have to at the end of your meal. At the more expensive restaurants you may wish to tip, but only if you have received exceptional service. At some coffee shops there are glasses at the till where you can deposit odd coins for staff if you wish to.

Below: exquisite food, lovingly prepared and elegantly served, at Friends Restaurant.

24; map p.135 C1
Picture yourself in British colonial Singapore – wicker birdcages, cane chairs and wooden tables. Joe's Oriental Diner looks the part as much as it tastes it. It serves a great range of dishes from Singapore, Malaysia and Thailand, and the brown-paper menus even carry a chilli rating (beware, these chilli ratings are serious, so anything sporting three chillis or more is very, very hot). The service is unobtrusive.

Yu

Burswood Entertainment Complex, Burswood Hotel, Burswood; tel: 08-9362 7551; Sun–Fri noon–3pm, 6pm–late, Sat 6pm–late; $$$$; bus: 24, 296

Offering some of the best Chinese cuisine in Perth, Yu's tends to take classic Chinese dishes and give them a contemporary twist. Its signature dishes include melt-in-your-mouth Szechuan sliced fillet steak, Portuguese stuffed crabs and Peking duck. Service is slick and the wine list is extensive.

Northbridge

EAST ASIAN
9 Fine Food

227–229 Bulwer Street, High-

gate; tel: 08-9227 9999; Tue–Sat 6pm–late; $$$; bus: 60; map p.134 B4

Chef-owner Muneki Song creates elegant, modern Japanese cuisine with a European influence. Bistro-style ambience.

FRENCH
Must Winebar

510 Beaufort Street, Highgate; tel: 08-9328 8255; daily noon–midnight; $$$; bus: 60

Enjoy a glass of wine in the funky front bar, or settle down for a serious French bistro-style meal in the restaurant. Has a 500-bottle wine list, and upstairs there is an ask-to-enter champagne lounge, where you can enjoy select bubbles by the glass (or bottle). Labels include Salon, Ruinart, Delamotte and heavy hitters such as Krug, Dom Perignon and Cristal.

INDIAN
Gogo's Madras Curry House

556 Beaufort Street, Highgate; tel: 08-9328 1828; Mon–Sat 6pm–late; $$; bus: 60

The Indian cricket team dine here when in town. Gogo cooks seriously good food,

with the menu extending beyond the obvious fare.

ITALIAN
Maurizio

235 Fitzgerald Street, Northbridge; tel: 08-9228 1646; Tue–Fri noon–3pm, 6pm–late, Sat 6pm–late; $$$; bus: 363, 60; map p.134 A4

Fine dining inspired by regional Italian food. Menus are created seasonally, but dishes such as the roast baby goat and braised rabbit are staples on the menu.

Veritas

484 Beaufort Street, Highgate; tel: 08-9328 9745; Tue–Fri noon–3pm, 6pm–late, Sat–Sun 8am–3pm, 6pm–late; $$$; bus: 60

This chic restaurant serves contemporary Italian and Mediterranean cuisine.

MODERN AUSTRALIAN
Jackson's

483 Beaufort Street, Highgate; tel: 08-9328 1177; Mon–Sat 7–10.30pm; $$$$; bus: 60

One of Perth's top places to dine. Chef-owner Neal Jackson likes to pair unusual combinations, such as apple risotto with grilled chorizo and seared scallops, and blue-cheese balls dipped in dark chocolate.

SOUTHEAST ASIAN
Little Saigon

489 Beaufort Street, Highgate; tel: 08-9227 5586; Tue–Sun 6pm–late; $; bus: 60

This little restaurant has a

Left: Perth offers some great waterside dining opportunities.

groovy red-and-white fit-out and serves authentic Vietnamese food. Try the prawns on sugar cane starter and the goat-and-eggplant curry. Good value and you can BYO.

Nahm Thai

223 Bulwer Street, Highgate; tel: 08-9328 7500; Wed–Sat 6pm–late; $$; bus: 60; map p.134 B4

This must be the best mod-Thai restaurant in Perth. The dishes are innovative and delicious – from the rich duck-and-lychee curry to the tangy galloping horses (mandarin topped with minced pork and chilli).

Subiaco

EAST ASIAN
Cheers

375 Hay Street; tel: 08-9388 2044; Mon–Fri 11.30am–2.30pm, 6pm–late, Sat 6pm–late; $; train: Subiaco; map p.132 B3

This authentic Japanese restaurant is hidden behind a group of shops on Hay Street. If you're with a group, make sure you ask for one of the traditional tables where you take off your shoes and let your feet dangle into the well under the table. Order a range of things to share.

INDIAN
Chutney Mary's

67 Rokeby Road; tel: 08-9381 2099; Mon–Tue 5.30pm–late, Wed–Sun noon–2pm, 5.30pm–late; $$; train: Subiaco; map p.132 B3

The fragrant smells wafting out of this Indian restaurant on the corner of Hay and Rokeby will entice you off the street. The thali plates are a popular lunch option, and at under A$15 are good value: choose between meat, fish or vegetarian curries; you'll also get rice, naan, dahl, soup and dessert.

ITALIAN
Funtastico

12 Rokeby Road; tel: 08-9381 2688; daily 8am–late; $$; train: Subiaco; map p.132 B3

If you can get upmarket casual, this is it. Favoured by folk-about-town for its good pastas and sensational pizzas, it has great alfresco seating.

Galileo

199 Onslow Road, Shenton Park; tel: 08-9382 3343; Tue–Sat noon–3pm, 6pm–late; $$$; train: Shenton Park

Serves elegant Italian cuisine, and definitely worth a visit. Those who like more unusual combinations will be kept happy, along with the more average palates. Not an easy balance to maintain, but they do it well. Staff are lovely and servings are generous.

MODERN AUSTRALIAN
Bistro Felix

118–120 Rokeby Road; tel: 08-9388 3077; www.bistro felix.com.au; Mon–Sat, noon–3pm, 6pm–late; $$$–$$$$; train: Subiaco; map p.132 B3

Bistro Felix is the place to come for refined Mod Oz cuisine. Chef Damien Young places emphasis on using produce in season, so the menu changes regularly, but expect lovingly executed dishes such as raviolo of

New to Western Australia is a website that can assist with your eating requirements. Eating WA is an online resource which provides punters with the opportunity to log on and post their own reviews of the restaurants they visit. You'll find star ratings as well as commentary, but as with all reviews, make sure you take them with a pinch of salt. You can search for restaurants by name, cuisine and location. See: **www.eatingwa.com.au**.

Above: elegance at Jackson's.

prawn, creamed corn with celery and sauce noire, and crisp confit of pork belly and vegetables 'en barigoule' with green tomato chutney. The wine list is huge and considered, with owner Jeremy Cariss managing to sweet-talk some producers into stocking their wines exclusively with him (other than at their own cellar doors).

Chapter One Brasserie

292 Hay Street; tel: 08-9388 1323; Tue–Sat noon–3pm, 6pm–late; $$$; train: Subiaco; map p.132 B3

It's easy to walk past this restaurant, but go in and dine and you'll be pleasantly surprised. The food is sophisticated – they can't take their rabbit pie off the menu – and it's followed by a choice of delicate desserts. There is a little courtyard area at the back, too.

Star Anise

225 Onslow Road, Shenton Park; tel: 08-9381 9811; Tue–Sat 6.30pm–late; $$$$; train: Shenton Park

One of Perth's best restaurants, located on the quiet shopping strip of Onslow Road. Chef-owner David Coomer changes the menu constantly, depending on what is good at the market.

Above: local produce at the Indiana Tea House.

There is an Asian influence, with crispy aromatic duck always on the menu, but in winter the menu reflects a comforting French style of cooking. Dessert is worth leaving room for, as it's always something interesting – such as balls of liquorice ice cream with slabs of Star Anise meringue.

The Subiaco Hotel
Cnr Hay and Rokeby streets; tel: 08-9381 3069; daily 7am–late; $$; train: Subiaco; map p.132 B3
Known just as 'The Subi', this pub-cum-restaurant is always busy, and deservedly so. The inventive, inspired food ranges from Moroccan seafood tagine with spinach and feta brik pastry and twice-cooked pork belly, with prawn and scallop caramel sauce and steamed rice cake. Booking advisable.
SEE ALSO PUBS AND BARS, P.98

The Witch's Cauldron
89 Rokeby Road; tel: 08-9381 2508; daily noon–3pm, 6pm–late; $$$; train: Subiaco; map p.132 B3
This restaurant has been on the Perth scene for longer than most people can remember. It is famous for its garlic prawns, steaks and seafoods. Not the most innovative cuisine, but reliable and loved by many.

Fremantle

EUROPEAN
George Street Bistro
73 George Street, East Fremantle; tel: 08-9339 6352; Tue 6pm–late, Wed–Sat 11am–late, Sun 9am–5pm; $$$; bus: 106
The walls are brightly coloured and adorned with artwork, the food robust German-Euro fare. There are some big flavours here, especially in the signature duck with braised red cabbage and sauerkraut. Very popular with locals.

FISH
The Mussel Bar
42 Mews Road, Fishing Boat Harbour; tel: 08-9433 1800; Tue–Sun noon–3pm, 6pm–late, Mon 6pm–late; $$; train: Fremantle
The atmosphere here is bright and cheerful during the day and more intimate at night. There is a strong wine list of over 175 wines and a creative menu that makes the most of the fresh local seafood, but includes some meat alternatives as well.

INDIAN
Maya
77 Market Street; tel: 08-9335 2796; Tue–Sun noon–2.30pm, 6pm–late; $$$; train: Fremantle
This multi-award-winning restaurant combines a modern, elegant interior and classic Indian food. The flavours range from intense to subtle – if you prefer heat, you'll find it, and if you like fragrant you'll be satisfied, too. Try the house speciality goat dish or the chilli whiting fillet and hot Tawa scallops.

ITALIAN
Limoncello
72 Marine Terrace; tel: 08-9335 1744; Tue, Sat 6–9.30pm, Wed–Fri noon–9.30pm, Sun noon–5pm; $$$; train: Fremantle
The fare at this shady café is authentic and tasty, with an emphasis on seafood. The dishes are simple yet full of flavour. The Italian owner has been producing excellent food from his eateries for many years.

MODERN AUSTRALIAN
Harvest
1 Harvest Road, North Fremantle; tel: 08-9336 1831; Tue–Thur 6pm–late, Fri noon–3.30pm, 6pm–late, Sat 7am–3.30pm, 6pm–late, Sun 7am–3.30pm; $$$; train: North Fremantle
Located in a quirky old cottage, with mismatched furniture, Harvest takes diners on an interesting culinary journey, exploring all sorts of

Right: the Indiana Tea House at Cottesloe Beach.

styles and flavours along the way. The food, however, is anything but chaotic. The breakfasts are delicious, and it's worth trying the rustic-style dishes at lunch and dinner, such as pine nut and sage-filled pork loin. Well worth a visit.

SOUTHEAST ASIAN
Sala Thai
22 Norfolk Street; tel: 08-9335 7749; daily 6pm–late; $$; train: Fremantle

Sala Thai offers authentic Thai flavours in a relaxed setting. The staff are warm and the food has a lovely fresh zing so typical of Thai. Good-quality ingredients and attentive service.

Cottesloe, Claremont, Swanbourne and Scarborough

MODERN AUSTRALIAN
Indiana Tea House
99 Marine Parade, Cottesloe; tel: 08-9385 5005; Mon–Sat 11am–4pm, 6pm–late, Sun noon–3pm; $$$; bus: 102, 103

This majestic building is hard to miss, as it sits perched above the sands at Cottesloe Beach. The style is colonial, but the food takes

inspiration from all over the world – from pasta to sushi. Probably not the best food on offer along the strip, but the experience is wonderful, as long as you get an ocean-side table.

Il Lido
88 Marine Parade, Cottesloe; tel: 08-9286 1111; Mon, Wed–Fri 6.30pm–late, Sat–Sun 8am–late; $$; bus: 102, 103

This funky café-cum-restaurant with its communal tables is directly opposite Cottesloe Beach, and they're happy for you to stroll in, sandy feet and all. The menu is exceptional, which is rare for a place with such a good view. Expect crab, lime and chilli linguine and Wagyu beef papardelle. Excellent wine list.

Oceanus
Challenger Parade, City Beach; tel: 08-9385 7555; Mon–Sat noon–late, Sun 8am–late; $$$; bus: 104, 105

This is the only restaurant on City Beach, and if it's high-class food you're after you'll find it here. Oceanus takes inspiration from modern Oz cuisine and specialises in seafood. Think grilled whole barramundi, cuttlefish, Catalan black rice and saffron aioli to get an idea of the sort of food the kitchen trots out.

Van's
1 Napoleon Street, Cottesloe; tel: 08-9384 0696; daily 6.30am–late; $$$; train: Cottesloe

This café epitomises the best that restaurants in Perth have to offer: a relaxed atmosphere, top-quality produce served in original ways, good wines, and great coffee to finish off. The duck spring rolls as an entrée are fantastic, the open sandwich with organic chicken and roast capsicum is a perfect light lunch, and

Approximate cost of main meal with a glass of wine:	
$$$$	A$50 plus
$$$	A$40–$50
$$	A$20–35
$	less than A$20

the dinner menu is mouth-watering.

Swan Valley and the Perth Hills

FRENCH
The Loose Box
6825 Great Eastern Highway, Mundaring; tel: 08-9295 1787; Wed–Sat 6pm–late, Sun noon–3pm; $$$$; by car

Award-winning French cuisine in idyllic surroundings. Top-quality ingredients are used, including organic herbs and veg grown in its on-site garden. Also has beautiful chalets where you can stay overnight.

MODERN AUSTRALIAN
Chester's of Heafod Glen
8691 West Swan Road, Henley Brook; tel: 08-9296 3444; Wed–Sun 10am–5pm; $$$; by car

The rustic charm of Chester's lends itself to a romantic night out or a happy family gathering during the day. There are wines made on site and the cuisine is award-winning. The signature dish is roasted red emperor wrapped in prosciutto and stuffed with a scallop and salmon mousse, topped with charred scallops in organic apple glaze.

Darlington Estate
39 Nelson Road, Darlington; tel: 08-9299 6268; Wed–Thur, Sun noon–3pm, Fri–Sat noon–3pm, 6pm–late; $$$; by car

The food at this winery restaurant is sublime. The style is European, with well-balanced flavours. The signature dish is a lamb shank wrapped in pastry. The wines are good and the views are beautiful.

Shopping

The shopping scene in Perth is very healthy, with new shops opening regularly, including big-name brands such as Gucci, Hugo Boss, Tiffany & Co. and Bally. Until 2007 Perth's only luxury brand was Louis Vuitton, which has occupied space on the exclusive King Street strip since 1997. The arrival of these heavy-hitters indicates that Perth's economy is flush and people are spending big. But it's not only international brands – small retailers with quirky flair are opening throughout suburbs such as Northbridge where rents are considerably lower than in the city or in the major shopping centres.

Antiques

Guildford's shops have the most variety – not by any means all fine, or even antique, but definitely interesting. Where else would you buy an ex-RAAF padded bag designed for parachuting crockery and cutlery? Opposite Guildford train station a dozen shops stock bric-a-brac and antiques. More are over the railway in Swan Street. Happy hunting can be done in Perth and Fremantle, too.

Several shopping malls and arcades lie between St Georges Terrace and Wellington Street, each with their own individual character. Trinity Arcade has three levels containing essential services, as well as treats such as rare books, antiques, fine menswear, jewellers and more. Piccadilly, Plaza and Carillon City are the other principal arcades. Many of the stores located within these arcades are not life-changing, but you will find some interesting buys nonetheless.

Fremantle Markets

Cnr South Terrace and Henderson Street; Fri 9am–9pm, Sat 9am–5pm, Sun 10am–5pm, Mon and public holidays 10am–5pm; train: Fremantle
There are a couple of shops here offering good finds.

Scurrs Antiques

769 Beaufort Street, Mount Lawley; tel: 08-9272 5181; Mon–Sat 10am–5pm; bus: 67, 21
This shop sells antique, Victorian, Edwardian and 1920s furniture brought over from the UK.

Arts

King Street, between Hay and Murray streets, is a culture strip, with several high-quality galleries and retailers.

Art Gallery of WA shop

Perth Cultural Centre, 47 James Street Mall; tel: 08-9492 6766; daily 10am–5pm; train: Perth; map p.134 B3
Stocks books on art, architecture and gardening, catalogues of exhibitions, and notepaper, prints and gifts.
SEE ALSO MUSEUMS AND GALLERIES, P.76–7

Creative Native

32 King Street; tel: 08-9322 3398; Mon–Sat 10am–5.30pm, train: Perth; map p.134 A2
Ethnic items.

Fremantle Arts Centre Shop

1 Finnerty Street, Fremantle; tel: 08-9432 9569; daily 10am–5pm; train: Fremantle
More Aboriginal style. This shop is crammed with ceramics, wood, glass, textiles and jewellery by WA artists.

Form

King Street Arts Centre, 357–365 Murray Street; tel: 08-9226 2255; Mon–Sat 10am–5pm, Fri until 8pm, Sun noon–5pm; train: Perth; map p.134 A2
Specialises in contemporary arts, with the usual ceramics, glass, etc, and also jewellery worked in titanium, gold, silver with Broome pearls and Argyle diamonds.

Department Stores

David Jones

622 Hay Street Mall; tel: 08-9210 4000; www.davidjones.com.au; Mon–Fri 9.30am–6pm, Thur until 7pm, Fri until 9pm, Sat 9am–5pm, Sun noon–6pm; train: Perth city; map p.134 A2

Left: shopping for antiques and bric-a-brac.

Sales seem to happen frequently – especially in the large department stores. Expect an end-of-financial-year stocktake sale, a pre-Christmas sale, an even better post-Christmas sale, plus end of season sales. Good savings can be found, especially on homewares such as bed linen, crockery, knives and cookware.

David Jones's flagship store faces onto the Hay Street Mall in the city, its large picture windows displaying of-the-moment designers. The store features imported Italian tiles which shine so brightly on the cosmetics floor you could just about do with wearing sunglasses. David Jones considers itself the more upmarket of the mall's two department stores, generally stocking more expensive options. Its food hall is excellent.

Myer
200 Murray Street; tel: 08-9265 5600; www.myer.com.au; Mon–Fri 9am–5.30pm, Fri until 9pm, Sat 9am–5pm, Sun noon–6pm; map p.134 A2
Myer fights hard to not be seen as David Jones's poor cousin. Its range is broad and slightly more affordable. Both stores stock a good range of Australian designers in dedicated sections, but often the floor stock can look tired. Myer has good sales and seems to have them often – mid-year, end of year, end of season and so on.

Right: Hay Street Mall.

Markets

For market updates see www.marketsonline.com.au.
E Shed Markets
Victoria Quay, Fremantle; Fri, Sun; 9am–5.30pm; train: Fremantle
A 100-year-old converted wharfside cargo shed with fresh produce, beautician, Australian bush goods, sheepskin, metal-craft, numerology, tarot and psychic readings.
Fremantle Markets
Cnr South Terrace and Henderson Street, Fremantle; Fri 9am–9pm, Sat 9am–5pm, Sun 10am–5pm; train: Fremantle; Has handmade and natural

organic produce, health food, cane-ware, pottery, finely crafted jewellery, painted T-shirts and clothing.
SEE ALSO FOOD AND DRINK, P.60
Station Street Markets
41 Station Street, Subiaco; Fri–Sun, Mon (public holidays) 9am–5.30pm; train: Subiaco; map p.132 B4
A wide range for sale, including small furnishings, clothes old and new, books, records, etc., as well as live entertainment in an open-air central courtyard.
SEE ALSO FOOD AND DRINK, P.61

Outback Style

Australian Geographic
Carillon Arcade; tel: 08-9322 8755; www.australian geographic.com.au; Mon–Sat, 9am–6pm, Fri until 9pm, Sun noon–5pm; train: Perth; map p.134 A2

Left: Carillon City.

leather gear, especially shoes. For northern-hemisphere visitors the exchange rate makes Australian leather shoes and boots especially good value.

R.M. Williams
Carillon Arcade, Hay Street; tel: 08-9321 7786; www.rmwilliams.com.au; Mon–Sat 9am–5pm, Sun noon–5pm; train: Perth; map p.134 A2

R.M. was a 'real' Aussie who became the 'bushman's outfitter' by providing solid and reliable kit, from boots, saddles and whips to hats and swags (bed-rolls) for rough Australian outback conditions. RM is now an international retailer with outlets across the Western world.

Quirky Finds

Black Plastic
120a Oxford Street, Leederville; tel: 08-9328 1236; Mon–Sat 10am–6pm, Sun noon–5pm; train: Leederville

An odd little gift shop with a huge range of quirky cards. Expect to find Jesus toys next to handbags and old movie posters.

Test Tube
6/595 Beaufort Street, Mount Lawley; tel: 08-9228 1118; Mon–Sat 10am–6pm; bus: 67, 21

This design-focused store sells a great range of gifts, or things simply to spoil yourself. The owners travel the world sourcing interesting design pieces – from jewellery to homewares, ties to beauty products. The fit-out won a commercial design award.

YoYo Buffalo
134 Oxford Street, Leederville; tel: 08-9443 4774; 10am–6pm, Thur until 8pm, Sun noon–5pm; train: Leederville

This store defies a simple

The eclectic stock here is certain to throw up an unusual, Australian-accented gift, such as soundtrack CDs of frogs croaking, or rock crystals that replace deodorant.

Mountain Designs
862 Hay Street; tel: 08-9322 4744; www.mountaindesigns.com; Mon–Sat, 9am–6pm, Fri until 9pm, Sun noon–5pm; train: Perth; map p.134 A2

Supplies professional-level outdoor clothing you could take up Everest.

Outback Red
Shop 8, Plaza Arcade; tel: 08-9325 5151; Mon–Sat 9am–6pm, Sun noon–5pm, train: Perth;

Bigger branches of **Purely Australian**, like that in Murray Street Mall, stock a wide range of Aussie icons, such as the Driza-Bone waxed stockman's coat and the fur-felt Akubra hat.

---

map p.134 A2

Rugged outdoor gear also figures large here, as well as the Ugg Boot, a sheepskin boot originally designed only for indoor 'slipper' use but now commonly seen on the streets.

Paddy Pallin
895 Hay Street; tel: 08-9321 2666; www.paddypallin.com.au; Mon–Sat 9am–6pm, Fri until 9pm, Sun noon–5pm; train: Perth; map p.133 E2

One of several stockists of hardcore outdoor wear on this part of Hay Street.

Rivers
Carillon Arcade, Hay Street; tel: 08-9485 0077; www.rivers.com.au; Mon–Sat 9am–6pm, Sun noon–5pm; train: Perth; map p.134 A2

With a young approach to casual country-style clothes for men and women, Rivers is strong on Australian-made

Right: R.M. Williams.

A referendum in 2007 saw WA vote against extended trading hours, which would have seen larger shops and suburban retailers allowed to trade more extensively on Sundays and late at night. Some wanted Perth to have more flexibility for the workforce who struggle to get to the shops in normal hours; others wanted to protect those who would end up working to accommodate the extended trading times.

Above: shopping in the sunshine.

tag – part rockabilly fashion, part retro, part club wear, and always unusual. Expect finds here you won't see anywhere else.

Shopping Centres
Carillon City
Between Hay and Murray street malls; tel: 08-9476 5888; www. carilloncity.com.au; Mon–Thur 9am–5.30pm, Fri 9am–9pm, Sat 9am–5pm, Sun 11am–5pm; train: Perth; map p.134 A2

Running between the Murray and Hay street malls is the warren of shops known as Carillon City arcade. There are over 140 stores, including a vast range of jewellers, fashion and food, and services such as travel agent, alterations, currency exchange and more. The mix

runs from bargain, cheap-as-you-like fashion through to high-end jewels.
Garden City
29 Riseley Street, Applecross; tel: 08-9316 7966; Mon–Sat 9am–6pm, Thur until 9pm; bus: 940, 881

Garden City is an older shopping centre, but several years ago enjoyed a dramatic facelift, and is now home to many quality retailers. As with many shopping centres, it's usually only national chains which can afford the rent. At Garden City you'll find both Myer and David Jones (see p.108–9), as well as a large range of fashion, homewares, sporting goods, jewellery and other retailers.
Karrinyup
Karrinyup Road, Karrinyup; tel: 08-9446 8454; Mon–Sat

8am–6pm, Thur until 9pm; train: Clarkson, bus: 425, 426, 423

Again, another older centre that has experienced a recent upgrade. There are some interesting retailers you won't find elsewhere, such as Crabtree & Evelyn, along with department stores Myer and David Jones (see p.108–9) with clothes, shoes and more luxurious consumables.
Westfield Carousel
1382 Albany Highway, Cannington; tel: 08-9458 6344; Mon–Sat, 8am–6pm, Thur until 9pm (food areas stay open late); bus: 220

A massive American-style shopping centre featuring cinema complex, large range of food options and many shops. Definitely not top-end, and gets incredibly busy.

Sports

Perth, like all of Australia, is sports-mad. The most popular spectator sports are Australian Rules Football during winter and cricket in summer. If you want to make friends with locals, especially men, you need to know what's going on, or at least be a keen student (and barrack for their team). Often the most diehard fans look like they've never thrown a ball or run a metre in their life. As for participant sports, the range is large, and during the better weather months there is a large range of competitions run just about every weekend, including ocean swims, triathlons, running and a large range of team sports.

Aussie Rules Football

Australian Rules Football is Perth's most popular spectator sport. AFL is a winter sport, running from March through to the Grand Final at the end of September. Western Australia has two national teams, the **West Coast Eagles** and the **Fremantle Dockers**, vying for local support. The Eagles are the older of the two teams, and have several premiership titles under their belt, the most recent being in 2006. The Dockers are yet to win a premiership; however, they are a strong team. Each plays home games at **Subiaco Oval** and local club games (WAFL–WA Football League) are played all around Perth. Memberships are sold to the teams, and this accounts for most of the 40,000-odd seats at Subiaco Oval, but each week a section is reserved for public ticket sales (at one end of the oval behind the goals). This allows fans of visiting teams, and those people who have not been able to secure, or who cannot afford, a membership to attend a game. Games that are sold out are broadcast live on free-to-air television.

Subiaco Oval
Between Subiaco Road and Roberts Road, Subiaco; tickets: 1300-135 915; www.westcoast eagles.com.au or www. fremantlefc.com.au; train: Subiaco; map p.132 B4–C4
Tickets are around A\$35 for an adult and can be purchased through www.ticket master.com.au or at the ground.

Left: Western Australia's two AFL teams in action.

Diving

Dive sites are located all around the WA coast, with many close to Perth. Local dives include Rottnest and Carnac islands, and extend as far as Dunsborough and Rockingham. You can also dive in the big tank at the Aquarium of Western Australia. Around Perth the diving season is October to May. Further north, at Coral Bay, Broome, etc, the season is much shorter.

West Australia Dive Centre

37 Barrack Street, Perth; tel: 08-9421 1883; www.watraveland dive.com; train: Perth; map p.134 A2

Runs diving courses and package tours as well as stocking all the equipment you'll require.

Horse-Racing

Perth has two racetracks, each just a short ride from the city centre. **Ascot**, with its outdoor bars and restaurants, is used for summer meetings. **Belmont Park** is on the river, with enclosed facilities to keep the punters warm and dry in the winter. Entry is generally free midweek, unless there is a special meeting, and remains cheap (around A$10) at weekends. Ascot's **Perth Cup**, on 1 Jan every year, is the racing and fashion highlight of the season. **Melbourne Cup** (the first Tuesday in November) is known as 'the race that stops a nation', and indeed it is. The biggest party on the day is at Ascot, and by the end of the day you'll find many bedraggled women in cocktail dresses and fascinators in pubs around town.

Subiaco Oval – dubbed 'the home of football' – celebrated 100 years in 2008. The stadium had a significant overhaul in the early '90s, but is due for redevelopment. The new home of football will still be in Subiaco, but the existing structure will be completely torn down.

Basketball

Perth Wildcats are WA's team in the National Basketball League. Their home base is at **Challenge Stadium**, but they often tour around Western Australia.

Challenge Stadium

Mount Claremont, Stephenson Avenue; tel: 08-9441 8222; www.wildcats.com.au; bus: 27, 28

Cricket

The **WACA ground** (Western Australian Cricket Association) is HQ of state cricket and venue for all important matches – state, championships,

Left: serious business at the WACA and a friendly game at the park.

---

international one-day, the new 20–20 format and Test matches. But high-standard matches featuring state players in their local club teams can be seen on ovals across Perth on summer weekends. The **Lilac Hill** ground in Guildford is one of the finest, worth a visit for its lovely rural setting by the river. Another is in the grounds of the University of WA in Crawley.

Lilac Hill

West Swan Road, Caversham; train: Guildford, then free shuttle bus

WACA Ground

Nelson Crescent, East Perth; tel: 08-9265 7222; www.waca.com.au; bus: red CAT; map p.135 D1

Cycling

Bicycles can be hired from **About Bike Hire**. There are numerous bike paths around the river, which make for a relaxing, picturesque activity. A comprehensive government site is www.dpi.wa.gov.au/cycling.

About Bike Hire

Cnr Plain Street and Riverside Drive; tel: 08-9221 2665; bus: blue CAT; map p.139 C4

Ascot

70 Grandstand Road, Ascot; tel: 08-9277 0777; www.perth racing.com.au; bus: 299 or check transperth.wa.gov.au for special arrangements on big race days

Belmont Park

Tel: 08-9470 8222; train: Belmont Park; map p.135 E4

Horse-Riding

Various horse-riding schools are located around Perth; to hire a horse for a good long ride you'll probably have to go out of town.

The Stables Yanchep

Yanchep Beach Road; tel: 08-9561 1606; train: Joondalup Hire a horse for a minimum of two hours and roam over trails and deserted beaches. Courtesy bus is available from Joondalup rail station if you reserve when booking. Fee is moderate.

Running and Jogging

Running is popular in Perth, and the 10km (6-mile) circuit around the bridges is well used. The biggest public run is the annual **City to Surf** (http://citytosurf.activ.asn.au), held at the end of August. Runners

start in the city on St Georges Terrace, making their way through Subiaco, Floreat and ending at City Beach. The run is 12km (7.5 miles), but there is also a 4km (2.5-mile) walk option, an 11km (7-mile) wheelchair option and a new half-marathon 21.1km (13-mile) option.

Soccer

Soccer is slowly gaining ground in Western Australia. The state team is **Perth Glory**, based at the Members Equity Stadium.

Members Equity Stadium

310 Pier Street, East Perth; tel: 08-6218 4203; www.perth glory.com.au; buses run especially during seasonal games, check http://transperth.wa. gov.au; map p.134 B3

Tickets can be purchased through the team's website. Local teams play on grounds across the city.

Surfing

Reliable conditions mean you can catch a wave all year in WA, though would-be surfers would be wise to check in first with the experts at Surfing WA (tel: 08-9448 0004; www.surfing

australia.com). Courses (for ages 8–70) are held at Trigg Beach, which with Scarborough has Perth's best surf. South of Perth, Yallingup and Lancelin are noted for bigger waves, and Margaret River is on the international circuit.

Indian Ocean temperature

Left: swimming the Rottnest Channel.

Burswood Dome
Burswood Entertainment Complex; tel: 08-9362 7777; www.burswood.com.au, bus: 296

Royal Kings Park Tennis Club
Kings Park Road, West Perth; tel: 08-9321 3035; bus: red CAT; map p.133 D2
Used for major competitions, such as the Davis Cup.

Triathlon

The sport of triathlon (swim, ride, run) is well supported in Western Australia, with the season of competitions running from October through to early May (www.triwa.org.au). Distances that athletes compete in vary, but the big ones to aim for are the **Busselton Half Ironman** in early May and the **Busselton Ironman** (www.busseltonhalf.com) in December. The Half distances are 1.9km (1.2-mile) swim, 90km (56-mile) ride and 21.1km (13-mile) run. The full Ironman distances are double this.

---

doesn't vary much in WA, but the wind chill does, and many surfers use wetsuits here. Surfing Australia will advise on shops that rent out suits and boards.

Adrift
5 Pascoe Street, Karrinyup; toll-free: 1800-094 480; www.adriftsurfing.com
Runs very reasonably priced surf tours and camps – one, two or three days – including transport to Lancelin, accommodation and meals, as well as four hours of lessons every day.

Swimming

Australian waters can be hazardous. In Perth, use a beach that's guarded by surf lifesavers and swim between the red-and-yellow flags that mark their surveillance area. Clean, well-maintained public swimming pools are located in most parts of Perth. The main one, used for championship events with indoor and outdoor pools, is at **Challenge Stadium**. During summer there are ocean swim competitions just about every weekend, check www.oceanswims.com. While some are club events, usually anyone is welcome to enter.

Challenge Stadium
Stephenson Avenue, Mount Claremont; tel: 08-9441 8222; bus: 27, 28

Tennis

Many tennis clubs in Perth will welcome visitor players. Suburban courts can also be hired for a fee; the details are usually posted on the fencing, and often a local deli collects money and distributes keys. The **Hopman Cup** is Perth's big international tennis tournament, played by mixed doubles in December/January at the **Burswood Dome.**

Left: cycling and jogging along the Swan River.

Each February around 2,000 swimmers depart the safety of Cottesloe Beach and swim to Rottnest Island. The swim is approximately 20km (12.5 miles), and you can opt to do it solo, in a duo or a team of four. The fastest are usually the solo swimmers, with the fastest time recorded being around the four-hour mark. A team of four average swimmers could expect to take seven to eight hours, depending on weather. All swimmers have a boat, support crew and a paddler, and sharks are asked not to attend. The first wave of swimmers leave the beach around 6.45am, so if you are in Perth in mid-February, check the date and go and wave the brave swimmers off.

115

Theatre

Diverse productions go on all year throughout the city, with a strong avant-garde scene supported by small companies and semi-professional groups. Perth has also begun to attract a good range of international productions, especially during February's Perth International Arts Festival *(see Festivals, p.54)*, where you can soak up everything from Korean versions of Shakespeare to Scottish plays about war. Perth has a well-patronised local scene, too, with several plays on at any given time. For more information on the performing arts, *see Music and Dance, p.80–83.*

Companies

Barking Gecko
180 Hamersley Road, Subiaco; tel: 08-9380 3080; www.barking gecko.com.au; train: Subiaco; map p.132 A2

This production company specialises in children's theatre. It also travels to schools to give workshops, and hosts workshops for ages 5–17, teachers and professionals.

The Blue Room Theatre
53 James Street, Northbridge; tel: 08-9227 7005;

www.pacs.org.au; train: Perth; map p.134 A3

The Blue Room is the trading name for the Performing Arts Centre Society, which is a membership-based, not-for-profit organisation. Formed in 1989, it offers WA performing artists a support network, and gives Perth audiences a wide range of eclectic shows.

Deckchair Theatre
179 High Street, Fremantle; tel: 08-430 4771;

www.deckchairtheatre.com.au; train: Fremantle

Deckchair is one of WA's most awarded companies, and focuses on West Australian stories wherever possible.

Perth Theatre Company
3 Pier Street, Perth; tel: 08-9323 3455; www.perth theatre.com.au; train: Perth; map p.134 B2

Perth Theatre Company has been producing professional theatre in Western Australia since 1983. The vision is about developing new West Australian theatre and supporting local artists. The company has a 'Writers' Lab' for playwrights and a programme called 'Umbrella!', which supports independent artists to produce their own work. PTC tours annually throughout regional Western Australian, visiting small, isolated areas as well as large cities and towns. PTC also tours nationally and internationally, and in 2008 staged the world premiere of an adpation of Tim Winton's *(see Literature, p.74) The Turning.*

Hill, this amphitheatre has
tiered, grass levels. You can
see the city skyline from the
top of the amphitheatre, and
in summer a series of concerts is held here, as well as
theatre productions.

Regal Theatre
Cnr Hay Street and Rokeby
Road; tel: 08-9381 5522; train:
Subiaco; map p.132 B3
The Regal is a heritage-listed
Art Deco building and attracts
a quirky range of shows,
often musicals, comedy and
other entertaining fare, gener-
ally not overly highbrow.

Spare Parts
Puppet Theatre
1 Short Street, Fremantle; tel:
08-9335 5044; www.sppt.
asn.au; train: Fremantle
As the name suggests, Spare
Parts is dedicated to puppetry. Its shows are written
for children, yet work on levels where adults get something out of them, too. Spare
Parts is considered one of
Australia's top puppet theatres – in 2008 it hosted the
World Puppetry Congress,
which saw a solid calendar
of public events attract
adults and children alike.
They also had a crack at setting a Guiness World Record
– a million puppets in one
place at the same time in
Perth's Concert Hall.

Yirra Yaakin
Aboriginal Theatre
3/9 Brook Street, East Perth; tel:
08-9221 9688; train: Claisebrook;
bus: red CAT; map p.135 C2
Yirra Yaakin is considered one
of Australia's premier Aboriginal theatre groups. They are
highly awarded and tell com-
pelling tales of historical and
contemporary Aborigines. If
you can manage to get to one
of their shows, it's worth it.

SEE ALSO ABORIGINAL CULTURE, P.27

For the biggest range of tickets
across theatre, dance and
music go to www.bocs
ticketing.com.au or call 08-
9484 1133. Most theatres use
this centralised service.

Theatres

His Majesty's Theatre
825 Hay Street, Perth; tel: 08-
9265 0900; www.hismajestys
theatre.com.au; train: Perth;
map p.134 A2
His Majesty's Theatre is a
grand building located on
the corner of Hay and King
streets in the city. Some see
it as an over-the-top, wed-
ding-cake-style building, but
you can't deny it has a
sense of grandeur. Inside,
marble staircases lead to
the higher levels of the
building, while inside the
theatre red carpet is the
theme, with small ornate
balconettes overlooking the
stage. Underneath the theatre there is a small space
where a series of contemporary performances happen,
called Downstairs at the
Maj.

SEE ALSO MUSIC AND DANCE, P.80

Playhouse Theatre
3 Pier Street, Perth; tel: 08-9323
3400; www.playhouse
theatre.com.au; train: Perth;
map p.134 B2
This theatre has been home
to many productions over the
years. While the theatre
doesn't have a dedicated
company attached to it, it's
never short of interesting productions, often from Aus-
tralian playwrights. Dance is
also often performed here.

Quarry Amphitheatre
Oceanic Drive, City Beach;
tel: 08-9385 8539; bus: 85
On the slopes of Reabold

The **West Australian
Academy of Performing Arts**
is regarded as one of
Australia's top training grounds
for actors, directors, producers
and anyone involved in the
performing arts. Entry is highly
competitive, and often it will
take several attempts before
admission is offered. WAAPA
(pronounced 'whopper') is part
of Edith Cowan University,
and boasts alumni such as
Australian actors Hugh
Jackman and Marcus Graham.

Transport

As the most isolated capital city in the world, it's hard to get to Perth by any environmentally friendly means. Generally visitors need to fly in, even if coming from another state in Australia, as the drive is long. The nearest capital city is Adelaide in South Australia, and that is 3,194km (1,996 miles) away. Once you are in Perth, you can access the main tourist sites easily by train. The trains are electric, fast, clean and new. Hiring a car is a good way to get around, too. Driving is easy in Perth as traffic is not heavy and it is easy to navigate; plus it gives you the flexibility to maximise your time in town.

Getting There by Air

INTERNATIONAL

Airlines are virtually the only way into Perth from abroad. Occasional cruise ships dock at Fremantle, but unless you have lots of time to spare on the journey, it has to be a plane. Most direct flights are routed via Singapore, and overnight stops there are a popular way to break the 20-hour European haul. Another popular route is via Dubai with Emirates, which divides the trip into two more equal legs. Fortunately there are plenty of airlines (listed below) serving Perth, and the runways are ready for the next generation of super-size jets.

Getting to Perth will almost certainly require you flying, and if not, some form of extensive rail or car travel will be the second option. Regardless how you get to Perth, it is worthwhile investigating how to offset your carbon footprint. www.carbonneutral.com.au is a good place to start, as is http://carbonoffsetguide.com.au.

Air New Zealand
Tel: 13 24 76; www.airnewzealand.com.au
British Airways
Tel: 1300-767 177; www.ba.com
Cathay Pacific
Tel: 13 17 47; www.cathaypacific.com.au
Emirates
Tel: 1300-303 777; www.emirates.com/au
Garuda Indonesia
Tel: 1300-365 331 or 08-9214 5101
Qantas
Tel: 13 13 13; www.qantas.com.au
Royal Brunei
Tel: 08-9321 8757; www.royalbruneiairlines.com.au
Singapore Airlines
Tel: 13 10 11; www.singaporeair.com.au
South African Airways
Tel: 08-9216 2200; www.flysaa.com
Thai Airways
Tel: 1300-651 960; www.thaiairways.com.au

DOMESTIC

If you're already in Australia there are direct flights from all other major cities with Qantas (see above) and Virgin Blue. New airlines make occasional forays into this tough market, but none has stayed the course for long. Virgin Blue usually has cheaper flights, but does not include in-flight catering or entertainment. On a five-hour flight from Sydney it could be worth paying the extra money for the distraction of being able to choose your own movies, television shows, radio and games.

Virgin Blue
Tel: 13 67 89; www.virginblue.com.au

AIRPORT

Perth Airport (www.perthairport.com) has separate terminals, about 5km (3 miles) apart, for domestic and international flights. If you are connecting with a flight, your airline will arrange shuttle transport. Otherwise taxis are the only link between the two locations.

FROM THE INTERNATIONAL TERMINAL

The only way of getting to and from the International Airport to the city centre is

Left: boarding a busy Transperth train.

run into central Perth bus station from the Domestic Terminal. Departures run from 5.30am–11pm, and from the/to the airport 6.25am–11.14pm; cost is minimal.

The Domestic Terminal is about 10km (6 miles) from the city centre, and a taxi will cost about A$25.

Getting There by Train

Railway buffs consider the Indian Pacific railroad one of the world's great rides. Well, it's certainly long. **Great Southern Railway** (tel: 13 21 47; www.gsr.com.au) operates the twice-weekly service into Perth from Sydney, via Adelaide and Kalgoorlie. The full journey of 4,352km (2,704 miles), much of it through the Nullarbor Desert, takes 64 hours and can be done in varying degrees of comfort, from sit-up-and-ache seats to private sleeper compartments.

The **Ghan Train** also runs from Adelaide to Darwin, via Alice Springs.

Getting There by Road

Coach services across the Nullarbor Desert from the eastern states have been abandoned, but one quirky option remains. You could

Flights to and around the north of Western Australia are regular and reliable, because of the stream of fly-in/fly-out workers at the mines. Qantas also services internal flights in WA.
Skywest
Tel: 1300-660 088
www.skywest.com.au

by taxi from just outside the terminal (beware: you may have to queue a long time) or by the shuttle bus. The International Terminal is 13km (8 miles) from the city centre and taxi fares are about A$30.

A 24-hour mini-bus service, **Perth City Shuttle** (tel: 08-9277 7958; www.perthshuttle.com.au; email: info@perthshuttle.com.au; A$15 from Domestic one-way, A$20 one-way International) meets all flights and runs to and from city hotels and the main train station. Booking is advised, especially if arriving after 9pm (it is essential to book return rides to the airport).

Right: Transperth Rail's Esplanade Station.

Fremantle Shuttle (tel: 08-9335 1614; www.fremantleairportshuttle.com.au) runs to and from the port city's hotels and backpackers (A$30) and private addresses (A$35), again 24 hours a day. There is an hourly service from 7am–7pm, but fewer buses at other hours. Call and book if arriving at the airport from 1–4am. Prices get cheaper the larger your group is.

FROM THE DOMESTIC TERMINAL

In addition to the shuttle services available from the International Terminal, public buses make the 20-minute

arrive from the north. **Greyhound Pioneer** (tel: 13 20 30; www.greyhound.com.au) runs long-haul buses from Adelaide to all major cities east and north, so travellers could take the scenic route, north to Darwin, thence to Kununurra, Broome, Exmouth and down to Perth.

DRIVING

Driving to Perth from the eastern states is considered a rite of passage for many Australians. Perth to Adelaide is 2,642km (1,642 miles); to Melbourne 3,375km (2,097 miles); to Sydney 3,902km (2,425 miles). Although there's a lot of featureless desert on the Nullarbor, you can make occasional diversions to the southern coast. Before considering the driving option take full safety advice from motoring organisations; and compare hire/fuel costs with internal flight deals.

Getting Around

BY BICYCLE

Cycling paths have been developed all around Perth, alongside the freeway, coast and even into the hills and cross-country. One path leads around the Swan in central Perth and all the way down to Fremantle. The **Perth Bicycle Network** (www.dpi.wa.gov.au/cycling) is a useful source of

> Transperth helps passengers with disabilities to access trains. Call 1800-800 022 an hour in advance and a customer service officer will meet you at the station. Prams and wheelchairs are easily accommodated on trains, ferries, CAT buses and the new green-and-silver Mercedes fleet of buses. But some older buses don't have extendable ramps; Infoline will give information on which routes do.

information. Maps are all available from bike shops, or the **Bicycle Transportation Alliance** (2 Delhi Street, West Perth; tel: 08-9420 7210). **About Bike Hire** *(see Sports, p.113)* rents bikes, double bikes, quadcycles – with trailers or baby seats.

BY BOAT

Cruising down the river is an excellent way to get to Fremantle, taking in views of Kings Park, Melville Water and the coves and beaches on both sides of the Swan. Both **Oceanic Cruises** (tel: 08-9335 2666; www.oceaniccruises.com.au) and **Captain Cook Cruises** (tel: 08-9325 3341; www.captaincookcruises.com.au) offer one-way or return trips, including tea/coffee and commentary. They take around an hour each way; Captain Cook

throws in a free wine-tasting on the return leg.

BY BUS

Transperth (InfoLine: 13 62 13) runs city buses, trains and the ferry. Transperth has an excellent website that can plan your journey for you, www.transperth.wa.gov.au.

Central city bus travel is free in the inner zone, which includes most parts visitors will want to see. Traffic jams are few, and buses are plentiful, so this is a quick way around town. The free service applies to all regular buses while they're in the central zone, as well as CATs. The free CATs (Central Area Transit) are distinctive buses – red, blue or yellow, depending on the route – linking the main tourist sights and running from early morning until early evening. Computer read-outs and audio messages at their dedicated bus stops tell you when the next CAT is due (generally within five minutes).

Most other bus routes head out of Perth in a radial pattern, which is fine for tourists heading for the beaches, Fremantle, etc. There are fewer services circling the city from suburb to suburb.

Tickets

Bus ticket prices depend on how many zones your journey covers. Pay the driver as you board the bus. Train and ferry tickets are bought at self-service machines.

DayRider tickets are good value for unlimited, day-long travel on all Transperth services after 9am weekdays and all day at weekends and on public holidays. Smart-

Left: light traffic and dedicated lanes makes cycling easy.

Right: open-top bus tours are a quick way to gain your bearings.

Rider electronic ticketing is a quick, cash-free system for use on any Transperth bus, train or ferry service.

BY CAR
Australians drive on the left, as in the UK. Cars are best for flexibility and convenience. If your driving licence is written in English you can use it in Australia for three months. An international driving permit will always be acceptable.

Remember there will be variations in road rules in Australia, and they can vary between states. WA's rules can be checked on the government website www.onlinewa.com.

A few pointers: seatbelts must be worn by driver and passengers; drivers must indicate lane-changing and never change lane in immediate vicinity of traffic lights or junctions. Perth's speed limit is 60kmh (about 30mph) unless otherwise signed. 'Local' streets will have 50kmh (30mph) signs; school zones are 40kmh (25mph). The top speed in the country is 110kmh (about 70mph) on open country roads where signed. On the freeway it's only 100kmh (about 60mph).

Major car hire firms in Perth are **Avis** (toll-free: 1800-812 808; www.avis.com.au), **Budget** (tel: 13 27 27; www.budget.com.au) and **Hertz** (toll-free: 1800-550 067; www.hertz.com.au). Others include **Thrifty** (tel: 1300-361 351; www.thrifty.com.au/wa) and **Hawk** (tel: 1300-361 351). All are at various locations accessible locations. Campervan and motorhome specialists include **Britz** (toll-free: 1800-331 454; www.britz.com.au),

CampaboutOz (tel: 08-9331 6500; www.campaboutoz.com.au) and **Wicked Campers** (toll-free: 1800-2468 69; www.wickedcampers.com), whose vans come multicoloured, with graffiti, for the young at heart.

Vehicle rental companies usually arrange a breakdown service.

BY FERRY
Perth's only regular ferry is also operated by Transperth, between **Barrack Street Jetty** on the north side of the Swan and **Mends Street Jetty** in South Perth. The ferry is a pleasant approach to the restaurants, bars, pubs and shops on the South Perth Esplanade and Perth Zoo.

BY TAXI
Hail taxis on the street, find them on a rank, or phone **Black and White** (tel: 08-9333 3333) and **Swan** (tel: 13 13 30). General rates are reasonable, a small flagfall charge followed by a rate per kilometre. Expect a long wait on Friday and Saturday nights.

BY TRAIN
Wellington Street is the central station, with an underground terminal for the

Mandurah line. Modern air-conditioned trains run south through Perth to Fremantle, north to Joondalup, and down the coast to Mandurah. It's a comfortable and efficient way to travel, especially during the day.

ON FOOT
Perth is small, the weather is usually fine and walking is more viable (and safe) here than in many cities. Equipped with sunhat, sunglasses, sunblock and a bottle of water, you're fit for anything. Free tours are available with City Perth volunteers. Meet them at the booth opposite the Commonwealth Bank buildings in Murray Street Mall, Mon–Sat 11am.

Right: Transperth's underground rail line.

Walks and Views

With districts often divided by rail lines and freeways, making it hard to wander seamlessly between neighbourhoods on foot, it has been joked that Perth is a city for cars; for a city with so many outdoor glories, it is not known for its easily accessible walks. However, this may be changing. In recent years, footpaths and bike paths have become more prevalent, and with the upcoming sinking of the Northbridge Link, this will undoubtably increase. In the meantime, there are still some peaceful and interesting walks to be found, and great vantage points to get that photo-perfect view over Perth.

City Views

Start: Barrack Street/Riverside Drive; map p.134 A1
End: Riverside Drive/Causeway; map p.139 D4

At the corner of Barrack Street and Riverside Drive, near the Swan Bell Tower, are the Supreme Court Gardens. These beautiful gardens play host to outdoor concerts in fair weather, but make for a worthwhile stop year-round. The gardens contain the **Supreme Court** and the City of Perth's oldest building, the original **Court House**. Now known as the Francis Burt Law Education Centre, it was built in 1836 and was the only building available for public meetings at the time of being built. It's also been a church, boys' school, law court and now houses a small museum (Mon–Wed, Fri 10am–2.30pm).

From the Supreme Court Gardens walk across to the **Swan Bell Tower** (see p.6). Heading east along the river's edge, you'll pass **Langley Park** on your left. Langley Park was created by land reclamation

Above: view over Perth.

between 1921 and 1935 and was originally used as an airstrip. Today, it's a popular spot to watch the **Australia Day** fireworks on 26 January (see Festivals and Events, p.54), and also plays host to games of polo, touring circuses and other events.

At the end of Langley Park on the riverside is **Point Fraser**. Recent works at Point Fraser have seen a new wetland created and connected by boardwalks. All along this path you get a wonderful view across the Swan River to South Perth, with the full height of the

Kings Park escarpment behind you (see box, right).

Kings Park Riverside and Tree-Top Walk

Start: Riverside Path, Kings Park; map p.137 D4
End: University of Western Australia; map p.136 A2

This walk offers lovely views over Perth's main green space in the city, Kings Park. Traverse the Tree-Top Walk for views over the canopy of trees and shrubs. The building glimpsed through the foliage on the left is the **Old Brewery**. Restored after years of controversy – Aboriginal people

Left: looking out over the city from the Swan Bells *(see p.6–7)*.

For one of the best views in Perth, head to the escarpment on Kings Park *(see Parks, p.89–91)*. From here you get the full effect of the sweeping Swan River as it wraps around the city and neighbouring suburbs. You can also see out to the Perth Hills and over the city. If you would like a drink with that view, head to St Martin's Tower at 44 St Georges Terrace. Catch the lift to level 33, where you'll find C Restaurant *(see Restaurants, p.101)*. C Restaurant is a revolving restaurant with floor-to-ceiling windows, so even if you don't plan to stay for a meal, grab a drink at the bar and enjoy the magnificent views going past.

claim this site is the sacred home of the Wagyl, a mysterious snake-like creature that created rivers by meandering over the land – it is now an upmarket complex of shops, restaurants and apartments. Depending on the time of day, there could be countless yachts on this stretch of river. You may also see the **Duyfken**, a replica of the ship in which the Dutch mariner Willem Jansz became the first European to record a landing in Australia, in 1606, 164 years before Cook's famous landing in Botany Bay.

From here, you can also visit the **University of Western Australia**, taking a 20-minute stroll through the bush. Native bush plants edge the path all the way, olive and sage-green rather than the lusher northern hemisphere emeralds. Some of the most distinctive are the banksias, with their cone-shaped flowers, palm-like zamias and grass trees, with their mop of spiky grass, which are known as 'the coconut of the southwest' because of the many uses

Aboriginal people make of them. Forest fires stimulate the growth of grass trees, blackening the fire-resistant trunk and lending them the common, if un-PC, name of 'blackboy'.

At the end of the park, turn left into Park Avenue, one of the most exclusive areas in the city. The administration buildings and residential colleges of the UWA line the avenue all the way to Winthrop Avenue. Of these, **St George's College**, with its crenellated towers and flag-pole, is the most picturesque. SEE ALSO CAFÉS, P.32

Northbridge Heritage Walk

Start: James Street; map p.134 A3
End: Newcastle Street/William Street; map p.134 B3
Though it hums at night, Northbridge by day is sedate. When colonists arrived, the area was swampy lakeland, but in the 1840s it was drained, and market gardens flourished in the rich soil. Building spread north from the river and central Perth,

Below: at the University of Western Australia.

and in 1861 the railway was taken through. After this, people began talking about 'north of the line' and eventually, Northbridge.

West along James Street, opposite Rosie O'Grady's is leafy **Russell Square**, a traditional meeting place for Aboriginal people and now, with its elegant town houses and new builds, a meeting place for everyone. Central to the rejuvenated square is the Pagoda artwork and bandstand, where concerts are regularly held. The cast-iron artworks represent WA's development and Northbridge's diversity: the granite galleon symbolises European influence; the pagoda the Asian community's impact on the area; the bronze snake and bearded dragon represent the natural environment; and a child's school bag, hope for the future. Fun and entertainment are represented by a bush hat, towel and sunglasses *(see picture, below)*.

Walk further along James Street, checking the **Bread-box** and **Fusebox** galleries on the way to Fitzgerald Street. Part of **Artrage**, an alternative arts organisation based near the **Western Australian Museum**, these galleries often have avant-garde shows on.

A right turn on Fitzgerald leads to St Brigid's Church and the **Piazza Nanni**, named in honour of Father Nanni, St Brigid's parish priest for many years. Built on land reclaimed when the Graham Farmer Tunnel cut through Northbridge, the granite piazza contrasts with the traditional red-brick and sandstone church buildings.

Look down onto the freeway emerging from the tunnel. This was Perth's biggest road-building enterprise in years. It cut a swath through Northbridge, taking out many old buildings, but also opening up new areas such as Piazza Nanni, and **Plateia Hellas** on Lake Street *(see p.14)*.

New streets bearing the names of notable local citizens reflect the international diversity of the area: Kakulas Court, Hoy Poy Street, Via Torre, Grigoroff Road and Zempilas Road among them.

Opposite Piazza Nanni is the start of the **Aberdeen Street Heritage Precinct**, with colourful houses and shops in a range of architectural styles. Many eminent early Perthites chose to live here, away from the bustle of the city. The shops and houses at the west end of Aberdeen were less grand, generally built as matching pairs in Federation Queen Anne, Bungalow or Free Classical style. Most striking of these (No. 182) is the bright blue-painted antique shop of Vincenzo Rizzo, built for Braddock's Dispensary in the 1890s (the name remains in the upper masonry).

A 'modern' Art Deco iron fence and gate, incorporating aircraft, cars and plant motifs, is a later addition to the well-balanced double-fronted No. 176. Victorian Italianate style is in evidence at Nos. 162 and 166, both dating from the gold boom and prosperous early 1890s.

Palmerston Street (north, off Aberdeen) is filling with new apartments. At the far end, the historic Union Maltings has been restored, turning rambling factories into new homes. Some units retain huge steel girders running through the walls, and solid jarrah floors. There's a small museum of artefacts and photographs of 1900s maltings operations, and sculptures made from industrial bits and pieces spread around the complex.

On the east corner where Newcastle Street crosses Palmerston is a small heritage precinct of cottages by the Perth architect Sir J.J. Talbot Hobbs. The small houses on Newcastle Street recall the start of Hobbs's career as an architect, when the population boom of the early 1890s inspired building in some unlikely locations. Hobbs built his cottages in modest Federation Bungalow style as investments to rent out. The

Below: one of the cast-iron works in the Pagoda.

Left: walking past The Brass Monkey pub *(see Pubs and Bars, p.97)* in Northbridge.

derful place to stop and enjoy views of the Indian Ocean, distant Rottnest Island, and the busy shipping lane into Fremantle.

Napier Street, alongside the north wall, will take you down to the ocean and Marine Parade. Turn to walk along the front, past pubs, cafés, restaurants and shops towards **Indiana Tea House**, the ideal waterside spot for an elegant lunch. This is the most popular part of **Cottesloe Beach**, with a paddling pool, volleyball courts and good swimming.

When returning to the station, you could live dangerously and walk through the attractive golf course along Jarrad Street. Look out for flying balls; you can keep all you catch.

SEE ALSO BEACHES, P.28–9; RESTAURANTS, P.107

contrast with his great works – such as the **WA War Memorial** in Kings Park, the Weld Club and the **Savoy Hotel**, couldn't be greater.

Follow Newcastle back to the entertainment area of Northbridge, via William Street. Upper parts of many Perth commercial establishments are original goldrush-era work. A newer one in striking Art Deco with an impressive vertical clock can be seen above a pizza shop where Newcastle meets William.

SEE ALSO MUSEUMS AND GALLERIES, P.77–8

Cottesloe Town and Beach Walk

Start/End: Cottesloe Station
Cottesloe is a popular and well-established small town with only 7,000 residents and many superior dwellings in a short coastal strip. The towering Norfolk pines you'll see on most streets have become something of an icon, a longlasting symbol of the town.

Many houses are in the turn-of-the-19th century 'federation' style, tastefully mixed in with modern developments.

At Cottesloe Station, cross the railway line on Jarrad Street and walk west towards the ocean. Jarrad Street will take you up to the Sea View Golf Course to the ocean, but stop short of the links and turn right on Broome Street to see the most splendid council offices in the state.

The Cottesloe Civic Centre is a 1911 Spanish-style mansion within Gothic balustraded garden walls, and set in spacious terraced gardens. Tycoon Claude de Bernales built the villa, wrapping it around the 1898 home of a one-time WA attorney-general. The grounds and walls date back to the original. As the buildings are in daily use by council staff, they aren't open to the public, but nobody will object if you wish to linger in the elevated gardens, a won-

Mundaring and Kalamunda are centres in an area rich in natural attractions. As well as local walks – in Fred Jacoby Forest Park, or on the abandoned Jorgensen Park golf course, there is the 1,000km (620-mile) Bibbulmun Track, which begins in Kalamunda. Meandering through the wild and picturesque countryside of the southwest, it is one of the world's great long-distance trails. It could take eight weeks to reach Albany on the south coast, but sections can be covered in shorter timeframes (there are cabins for overnight stops). For options, including single-day walks without a pack, contact the Bibbulmun Track Foundation (tel: 08-9481 0551; www.bibbulmuntrack.org.au).

Wine Country

Australia's largest state boasts nine wine-growing regions and over 350 wineries, almost entirely concentrated in its southwest corner. Though they account for just 3 percent of Australia's wine production, they produce 20–30 percent of the country's premium vintages. Wine is big business in WA, and most wineries will have a cellar door where you can try and buy. There has been a lot of effort put into making cellar doors attractive; some are nothing short of splendid. Tastings are mostly free, although on more expensive wines you may have to pay a small fee, usually around A$2–3, to be waived if you purchase.

Great Southern

Adjacent to Margaret River, the Great Southern region is noted for Cabernet wines of deep colour and intense flavour, as well as for Rieslings and Chardonnays. It also produces a small amount of high-quality Shiraz, with some promising Pinot also emerging. Its estates include Ferngrove, Alkoomi, Goundrey, Frankland and Howard Park. See: www.greatsouthern wines.com.au

Alkoomi

1141 Wingebellup Road, Frankland River; tel: 08-9855 2229; www.alkoomi wines.com.au; daily; by car
Alkoomi's wines are held in great esteem, with the cool climate of the region lending itself to sumptuous reds and a beautiful Riesling.

Ferngrove

Ferngrove Road, Frankland; tel: 08-9855 2378; www.ferngrove. com.au; daily 10am–4pm; by car
Ferngrove's first vintage was produced in 2000, and it hasn't looked back. Known for its estate-grown, cool climate wines, Ferngrove continues to win awards, including in 2005 when its winemaker, Kim Horton, won Australia's Young Winemaker of the Year. Ferngrove also has on-site chalet accommodation.

Howard Park

Scotsdale Road, Denmark; tel: 08-9848 2345; www.howard parkwines.com.au; daily 10am–4pm; by car
Howard Park is worth a visit. Its wines are highly awarded and have been commended Australia-wide. Special tours of the winery are available if you arrange it in advance.

Margaret River

By far the most prestigious and well-known region is Margaret River. Renowned as a producer of robust Cabernets since the 1970s, it has since forged a reputation for crisp white wines, notably Chardonnay and Semillon Sauvignon Blanc blends. Its Shiraz has also won acclaim, and Merlot is widely used as a blend component. Home to estates such as Evans and

Below: the Australia flag flies proudly over the Voyager Estate.

River; has an excellent display of modern art in the grounds, and an extensive Aboriginal art gallery. The restaurant is a must-do. They are known for their sparkling wines, and have small plantings of interesting grapes, such as Tempranillo.

Voyager Estate
Stevens Road, Margaret River; tel: 08-9757 6354; www.voyagerestate.com.au; daily; by car

Voyager Estate's entrance and grounds are as impressive as its wines. White-washed Cape York-style walls meet rolling lawns, roses and beautiful buildings. You can't miss the gigantic Australian flag in the driveway. It is known for its whites, and the restaurant is good, too.

Peel

Close to Perth is the Peel region, known for its Shiraz and Cabernet Sauvignon. It is not one of the bigger regions,

---

Tate, Cullen, Voyager, Vasse Felix, Wise, Leeuwin and Pierro, and with more than 70 cellar doors, the region is a mecca for international wine-lovers. See: www.mrwines.com.

For organised tours, contact **Milesaway Tours** (tel: 08-9754 2929) or **Taste the South Winery Tours** (tel: 0438-210 373). If you prefer to visit the wineries independently, many of the best ones are on Caves Road and the roads leading off it between Yallingup and Gracetown. All the wineries are well signposted. You'll never get around to all of them, so pick a few that take your fancy and do them well.

Cullen
Caves Road, Cowaramup; tel: 08-9755 5277; www.cullen wines.com.au; daily; by car

Specialises in quality wines from single-vineyard sites. Vanya Cullen's Diane Madeline Cabernet Merlot was recently classified in the Exceptional category of Langton's fourth classification of Australian wines.

Leeuwin Estate
Stevens Road, Margaret River; tel: 08-9759 0000; www.leewin estate.com.au; daily; by car

Family-operated winery famous for its Art Series Chardonnays, but it doesn't produce a bad wine. There is a large grassed area where each year the Leeuwin Concert is held – this black-tie affair is one of 'the' events of the year.

Moss Wood
Metricup Road, Willyabrup; tel: 08-9755 6266; www.moss wood.com.au; by appointment; by car

One of WA's great wine estates, producing excellent Pinot Noir, Chardonnay, Cabernet Sauvignon and Semillion. Go if you can.

Pierro
Caves Road, Willyabrup; tel: 08-9755 6220; www.pierro.com.au; daily; by car

Family-owned boutique winery noted for its Chardonnays. Those in the know love it.

Vasse Felix
Cnr Caves and Harmans roads, South Cowaramup; tel: 08-9756 5050; www.vassefelix.com.au; daily; by car

First commercial winery to be established in Margaret

If you plan to visit any of these areas, you will need to drive, or be driven. There are some wine-tasting tours, but if you want to go your own speed or off the beaten track, you are best off hiring a car and nominating a designated driver. Police do patrol these roads, and they conduct random breath-testing to determine if drivers are over the blood alcohol limit. Being over 0.05 blood alcohol means you will be fined, and possibly have your licence suspended. You also will not be allowed to drive any further, and if your passengers have also been drinking, you'll be forced to abandon your car. The best bet is just not to drink at all.

but still produces good wines and is nice and close to Perth, making it handy for a day trip.

Peel Estate

290 Fletcher Road, Karnup; tel: 08-9524 1221; www.peel wine.com.au; daily 10am–5pm; by car

Established in 1973, this winery is certainly one of the older ones in WA. The first wines planted were Shiraz, and then Chenin Blanc and Zinfandel in 1976. Others followed, and the winery is still going strong. The cellar door is a pretty, wisteria-covered place, and they encourage you to order ahead for picnics. Tasting platters are also available.

Pemberton and Manjimup

Pemberton region enjoyed rapid growth in the 1990s, and is noted mainly for its Chardonnay, with some Merlot and Cabernet Sauvignons also garnering acclaim. Its estates include Salitage, Mountford and Picardy. See: www.pembertonwine.com.au.

Manjimup is dominated by Chardonnay, Cabernet Sauvignon and Merlot plantings, and in the Blackwood Valley the main reds are Cabernet Sauvignon and Shiraz. Geographe is noted for the softer character of its Cabernets.

Capel Vale

Lot 5 Mallokup Road, Capel; tel: 08-9727 1986; www.capel vale.com; daily; by car

While not handily surrounded by a whole heap of other wineries like those in Margaret River, Capel Vale is still worth a pit stop.

Killerby

Lakes Road, Stratham; tel: 1800-655 722; www.killerby.com.au; daily 10am–5pm; by car

Known for its Chardonnay, Killerby also has a vineyard in

Above: a golden vine in the Swan Valley.

Margaret River. They are a founding wine family, and the family still owns the vineyards.

Picardy

Cnr Vasse and Eastbrook Roads, Pemberton; tel: 08-9776 0036; www.picardy.com.au; by appointment; by car

The Pannell family are one of the region's stalwarts. Producing Chardonnay, Pinot Noir, Shiraz and Merlot/Cabernet varieties, all their fruit comes from their Pemberton property. Well respected.

Salitage

Lot 3, Vasse Highway, Pemberton; tel: 08-9776 1195; www. salitage.com.au; daily; by car

John and Jenny Horgan are behind Salitage and are key players in the WA wine scene, having much to do with getting the vaulted Margaret River region going in the 1970s. Salitage uses only French oak barriques when barrel-ageing its wines. Try its Chardonnay. Salitage also has on-site accommodation.

Perth Hills

The Perth Hills area has been cultivating grapes since colonial days, but was only gazetted as a wine region in 1999. It now has 16 wineries and 13 cellar doors, two of note being Darlington Estate and Millbrook. While both fall into the 'Perth Hills' wine

region, they are a fair drive apart, Darlington Estate being east of the city, and Millbrook southeast. Both have excellent restaurants, for which you need to book.

Darlington Estate

Lot 39 Nelson Road, Darlington; tel: 08-9299 6268; www.darlingtonestate.com.au; Wed–Sun and public holidays noon–5pm, Fri–Sat dinner 6.30pm–late; by car

On Friday night, a very good jazz trio plays.

Millbrook Winery

Old Chestnut Lane, Jarrahdale; tel: 08-9525 5796; www. millbrookwinery.com.au; light lunches: Mon–Tue, restaurant lunches: Wed–Sun; by car

Striking boutique winery in picturesque setting.

Swan Valley

Located roughly 30 minutes east of the CBD. You can pick up a food-and-wine trail map from the Swan Valley tourism office located in the historic Guildford courthouse (cnr Meadow and Swan streets, Guildford; tel: 08-9379 9400; www.swan valley.com.au; daily 9am–4pm). The trail takes in 32km (20 miles) of scenic driving, as well as over 80 wineries, breweries and restaurants. Driving in the Swan Valley is easy, as there are really only two main roads once you get out there. To get there from

Perth, head out along Great Eastern Highway, taking the bypass, and then just follow the signs until you get to Guildford. On Guildford's main drag you will see a turn across railway tracks which is clearly signposted to the Swan Valley. As you make this turn, the Visitor Centre will be on your right; stop here for one of the trail maps.

The valley is renowned for its fortified wines, Verdelhos, Shiraz and Cabernet. Growing consumption at home and abroad led countless landowners to turn their hectares over to vines in the 1990s, and the resulting glut has made everyday wine-drinking extremely affordable. These bargains, known as 'cleanskins' because they are usually unlabelled, can only be found in bottle-shops. Don't expect such low prices at the vineyards, where you will find handmade wines of superior depth, style and quality.

The chance to try a wide range of wines and styles is enhanced in the Swan Valley by the diversity of vineyards, large and small, grand and humble.

Houghton
Dale Road, Middle Swan; tel: 08-9274 9540; www.houghton wines.com.au; daily; by car
A valley stalwart, established in 1836 by three army officers, Houghton is WA's largest commercial winery. Like Sandalford, it has an extensive stable of wines, souvenirs and a restaurant, and it even holds concerts under the trees. Its most famous winemaker was Jack Mann, whose family now run Mann Wines. During his 51 vintages with Houghton he produced their White Burgundy, Australia's best-selling bottled wine.

Houghton Wines
Dale Road, Middle Swan; tel: 08-9274 9540; www.houghton-wines.com.au; daily; by car
A rustic drive off the Great Northern Highway into the extensive grounds ends under jacaranda trees, heavy with blue blossom in spring.

Lancaster Wines
5228 West Swan Road; tel: 08-9250 6461; www.lancaster wines.com.au; daily; by car

Most cellar doors are open from 10am daily, and will close around 5pm. Also, don't be put off by cellar doors that only open by appointment – people are very friendly, and only too keen to show you their wines. There is never any obligation to buy wine, either.

With its unmade road and makeshift tasting shed, Lancaster Wines looks fairly humble, yet has some of the valley's oldest vines and most knowledgeable staff. Lancaster offers all the grape types that grow best in Swan Valley (Shiraz, Cabernet Sauvignon, Verdelho, Chenin Blanc and Chardonnay), including an Old Vines Shiraz, plus a late-picked Chenin dessert wine. Good, strong local cheese is served, too.

Sandalford
3210 West Swan Road; tel: 08-9374 9300; daily; by car
One of the grand ones, although most of its award standard wine is sourced from its estate in the Margaret River wine area. Its much smaller Swan Valley property was started in 1840 by John Septimus Roe, WA's first surveyor-general. It has won awards for its Cabernet Sauvignon and produces one, the Prendiville Reserve, which will reward the patience of anyone willing to cellar it for up to 25 years.

Talijancich
26 Hyem Road; tel: 08-9296 4289; Sun–Fri; by car
A must for its fortified wines – tawny and vintage port, Muscat and Tokay. It hosts an annual international vintage Verdelho-tasting to swell appreciation of this grape. Its own Verdelho is superb, as is the Old Vine (1932) Shiraz.

Left: in the Houghton winery.

Atlas

The following streetplan of Perth makes it easy to find the attractions listed in the A–Z section. The selective index to streets and sights will help you find other locations throughout the city

Map Legend

Freeway	Bus station
Main roads	Airport
Minor roads	Tourist information
Footpath	Sight of interest
Pedestrian area	Cathedral / church
Notable building	Statue / monument
National Park	Tower
Hotel	Summit
Urban area	Lighthouse
Non urban area	Beach
Cemetery	Viewpoint

WEMBLEY   LEEDERVILLE

Barrett St

Gregory St

Connolly St

Joseph St

McCourt St

Avenue

Street

Street

Street

Cambridge Street

Station

St John of God
Health Care

McCourt Street

Tate Street

St Leonards

Biencowe

Northwood

West Leeder
Railway Sta

Salvado Road

Railway Parade

Haydn Bunton Dr.

4

JOLIMONT

Mere View Way

Juniper Bank Way

Harborne St

Roydhouse St

Station St

Wexford St

Subiaco
Square

KITCHENER
PARK

SUBIACO
OVAL

Flood St

Upham St

Flood St

Subiaco
Railway
Station

Market
Square

Price Street

Carter La

Centro Ave

Railway Road

Roberts Road

St

Road

Ave

65

Lords
Sport Stadium

Subiaco
Pavillion
Markets

Catherine St

York

Axon

Street

Townshend

Ellen St

May

*Quest
Subiaco*

Hay Street

Station
Street
Markets

Alvan St

Regal
Theatre

3

Hay   Street

Subiaco
Village

Hay
St

St

Forrest   St

Churchill Avenue

SUBIACO

Road

Churchill Avenue

Olive St

Troy Terrace

Robinson Terrace

Barker Road

Street

Barker Rd

Stubbs Terrace

King Edward
Memorial Hospital
for Women

Loretto St

Raphael St

Denis

Rowland

Rokeby

Park Street

Axon

St

Park St

Olive St

Avenue

Railway Road

Road

Bagot Road

Subiaco
Library

Bagot Road

Bedford

Kings Rd

Francis St

2

THEATRE
GARDENS

Subiaco
Museum

Hensman

Lawler St

Douglas Ave

Street

Subiaco
Theatre
Centre

RANKIN
GARDENS

Rupert St

Salisbury St

Robinson St

Proclamation St

Road

Hamersley Road

Hamersley Road

Derby

Federal

Road

St

Redfern

View
St

Browne
St

Road

Street

Union
Street

Rawson St

Campbell St

Rokeby Road

Rupert Street

Chester St

Kershaw St

Townshend

Thomas Street

Heytesbury

Road

Road

Heytesbury Road

Federal

Hensman

Salisbury St

Gloster Street

View
Street

Gloster St

Union Street

Coolgardie St

Duke St

Rupert Street

Nicholson Road

64

Nicholson Road

Derby

Waverley St

William St

St

Hensman Rd

Rosalie St

Street

Arthur St

Rokeby Road

61

KINGS

Road

Stanmore St

Henry
St

Keightley Road W

Keightley Road E

Thomas

Subiaco
Lodge

May   Drive

Derby

Waverley Street

Stanmore Street

Cross
Street

Cullen St

Hensman Rd

Rosalie St

Austin

Thomas

Saw Ave

| 0 | | 400 m |
| 0 | | 400 yards |

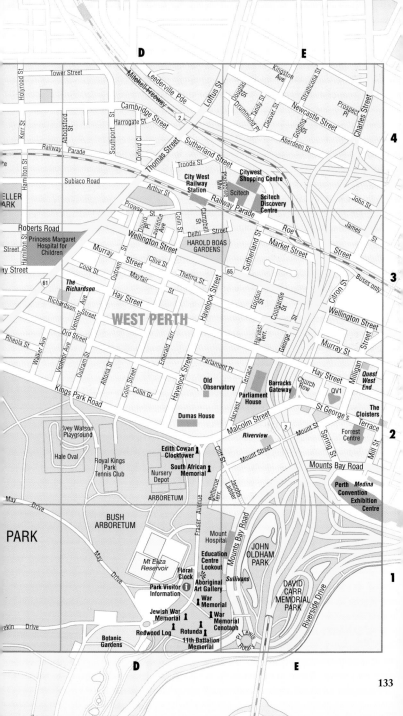

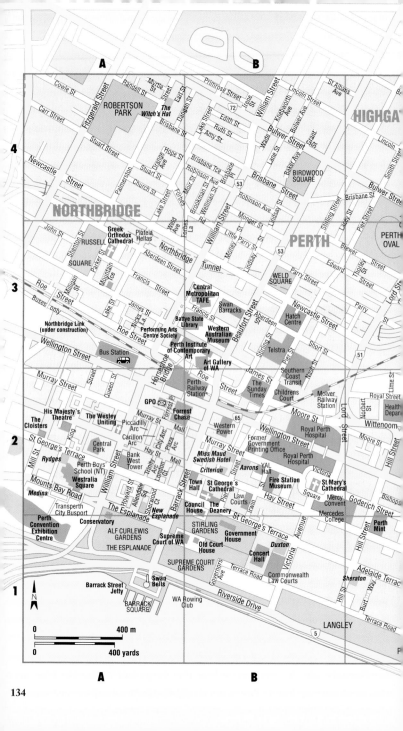

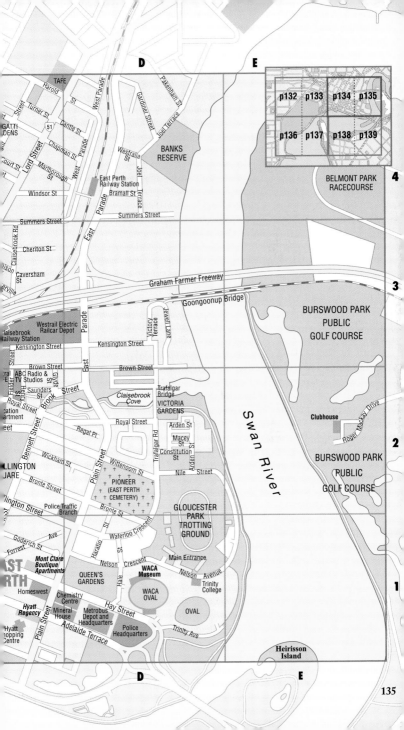

4

BELMONT PARK
RACECOURSE

TAFE

Harold

Turner St

St

West Parade

Cantle St

GATTI
DENS

51

Chapman Parade

Pakenham St

Joel Terrace

Gardiner Street

Lord Street

Marlborough St

West Parade

Westralia St

BANKS
RESERVE

ourt St

Windsor St

East Perth
Railway Station

Bramall Terrace

Joel Terrace

Summers Street

Summers Street

Summers Street

Claisebrook Rd

Cheriton St

East Parade

son
erville

Caversham
St

Graham Farmer Freeway

3

Goongoonup Bridge

BURSWOOD PARK
PUBLIC
GOLF COURSE

Westrail Electric
Railcar Depot

Claisebrook
Railway Station

Kensington Street

Kensington Street

East Parade

Victory Terrace

Jewell Lane

Brown Street

Brown Street

Brown Street

ral
E

ABC Radio &
TV Studios

Fielder St

Royal Street

Saunders
St

Brook   Street

Trafalgar
Bridge

cation
partment

Claisebrook
Cove

TRAFALGAR RD

VICTORIA
GARDENS

Clubhouse

Roger Mackay Drive

eet

Bennett Street

Regal Pl.

Royal Street

Arden St

S w a n   R i v e r

2

BURSWOOD PARK
PUBLIC
GOLF COURSE

LLINGTON
UARE

Wickham St

Plain Street

Wittenoom St

Macey
St

Constitution
St

Bronte Street

PIONEER
(EAST PERTH
CEMETERY)

Nile   Street

Arden

llington Street

Bronte St.

Police Traffic
Branch

Goderich St

Ave

Haratio
St

Waterloo Crescent

GLOUCESTER
PARK
TROTTING
GROUND

1

Forrest St

Mont Clare
Boutique
Apartments

Nelson

Crescent

Main Entrance

Nelson   Avenue

AST
RTH

Homeswest

QUEEN'S
GARDENS

Hale St

WACA
Museum

WACA
OVAL

Trinity
College

Hyatt
Regency

Chemistry
Centre

Mineral
House

Hay Street

OVAL

Hyatt
hopping
Centre

Plain Street

Metrobus
Depot and
Headquarters

Adelaide Terrace

Police
Headquarters

Trinity Ave

Heirisson
Island

D E

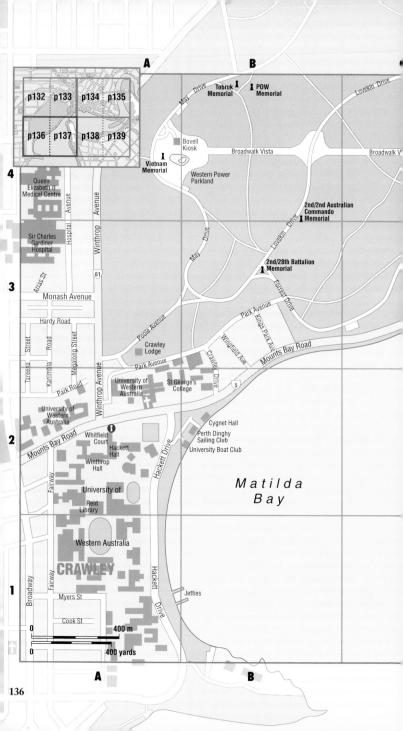

A

B

May Drive

Tobruk
Memorial

POW
Memorial

Lovekin Drive

Bovell
Kiosk

Broadwalk Vista

Broadwalk V

Vietnam
Memorial

Western Power
Parkland

4

Queen
Elizabeth II
Medical Centre

Hospital Avenue

Winthrop Avenue

2nd/2nd Australian
Commando
Memorial

Lovekin Drive

Sir Charles
Gardiner
Hospital

61

2nd/28th Battalion
Memorial

May Drive

Forrest Drive

3

Arras St

Monash Avenue

Hardy Road

Poole Avenue

Park Avenue

Kings Park Avenue

Mounts Bay Road

Tareela Street

Kanimbla Road

Megalong Street

Park Road

Crawley
Lodge

Wingfield Ave

Park Avenue

Crawley Drive

University of
Western
Australia

St George's
College

5

Winthrop Avenue

2

University of
Western
Australia

Mounts Bay Road

Whitfield
Court

Hackett
Hall

Winthrop
Hall

University of

Reid
Library

Hackett Drive

Cygnet Hall

Perth Dinghy
Sailing Club

University Boat Club

*Matilda
Bay*

Fairway

Western Australia

CRAWLEY

1

Broadway

Fairway

Myers St

Cook St

Hackett Drive

Jetties

0 ____ 400 m

0 ____ 400 yards

A

B

136

Forrest Drive

Pioneer
Women's
Memorial

Lotterywest
Federation Walkway
(Tree-Top Walk)

Botanic
Gardens

Bessie Rischbeith
Memorial

Duyfken

DNA Observation
Tower

WATER
GARDENS

Old Swan
Brewery

Point Lewis

The   Narrows

Narrows

Bridge

Mill Point

Point Belches

Water Ski Area
(Commercial)

Mill
Point
Cl.

Jetty

Mill Point Road

Melville
Pl.

South Perth Esplanade

Queen St.

Roe
Memorial

Drummond
Memorial

Water Ski
Area

Stirling St.

Frasers
Lane

rrest Drive

Mounts Bay Road

Scott St.

Stone Street

Mill Point Road

Ferry
St.

Harper Terr.

Mill Point Road

Ments St.

rry Point

Swan River

Judd Street

Bowman Street

WINDSOR
PARK

Lyall Street

Labouchere Road

Hardy Street

Melville Parade

Charles Street

Melville Water

Richardson Street

RICHARDSON
PARK

Amherst
St.

Kwinana Freeway

ROYAL PERTH

GOLF CLUB

N

4

3

2

1

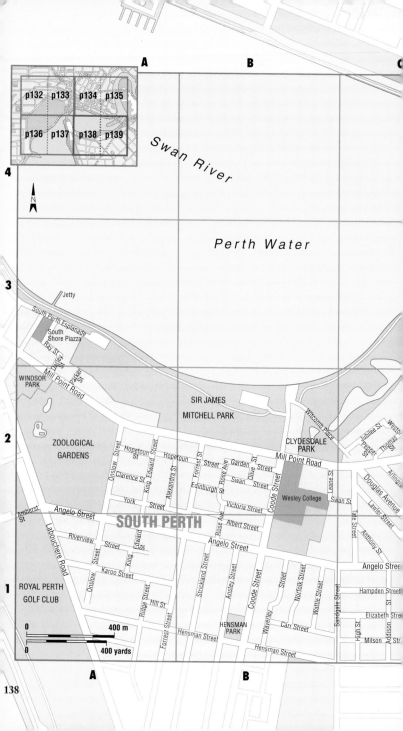

A

B

C

p132 p133 p134 p135

p136 p137 p138 p139

4

N

Swan River

Perth Water

3

Jetty

South Perth Esplanade

South Shore Piazza

Ray St

Dunkley St

Parker St

Mill Point Road

WINDSOR PARK

SIR JAMES MITCHELL PARK

Witcomb Place

2

ZOOLOGICAL GARDENS

CLYDESDALE PARK

Mill Point Road

Jubilee St

Westey

Pepper St

Thomas

Onslow Street

Hopetoun St

Hopetoun Street

Forrest St

Garden St

Olive St

Street

Leane St

Douglas Avenue

King Edward Street

Alexandra St

Rose Ave

Swan Street

Arling

Clarence St

Edinburgh St

Street

Lawler Street

York Street

Victoria Street

Wesley College

Swan St

Anthony St

Tate Street

Amherst St

Angelo Street

SOUTH PERTH

Albert Street

Rose Ave

Angelo Stree

Labouchere Road

Riverview Street

Edward St

Angelo Street

Angelo Street

1

ROYAL PERTH GOLF CLUB

Onslow Street

King Street

Karoo Street

Strickland Street

Ansley Street

Coode Street

Street

Norfolk Street

Wattle Street

Sandgate Street

Hampden Street

Ridge Street

Hill St

Waverley

Carr Street

High St

Elizabeth St

St

Addison

Forrest Street

Hensman Street

HENSMAN PARK

Hensman Street

Milson

Str

0   400 m

0   400 yards

A

B

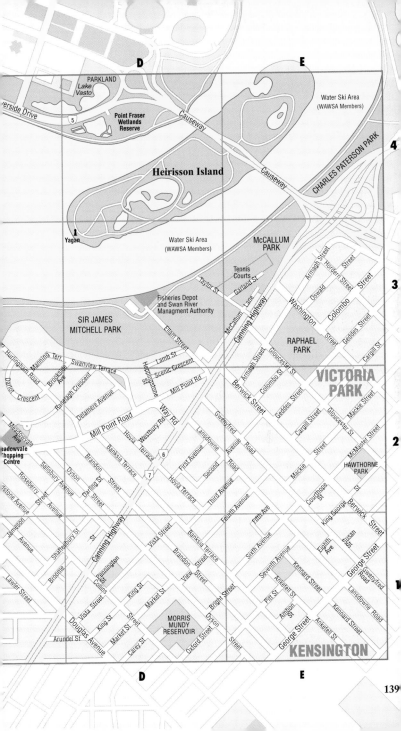

Riverside Drive

PARKLAND
Lake
Vasto

Point Fraser
Wetlands
Reserve

Causeway

Water Ski Area
(WAWSA Members)

4

Heirisson Island

Causeway

CHARLES PATERSON PARK

Yagan

Water Ski Area
(WAWSA Members)

McCALLUM
PARK

Tennis
Courts

Taylor St

Garland St

3

Fisheries Depot
and Swan River
Managment Authority

McCallum Lane

Canning Highway

Washington Street

Armdah Street

Hordern Street

Oswald

Colombo Street

Geddes Street

SIR JAMES
MITCHELL PARK

Elham Street

Lamh St

RAPHAEL
PARK

Armdah Street

Gloucester St

Cargil St

Huringham Road

Manning Terr.

Swanview Terrace

Heppingstone St

Scenic Crescent

Mill Point Rd

Colombo St

Geddes Street

**VICTORIA
PARK**

Darlot Crescent

Brooksie Ave

Ranelagh Crescent

Delamere Avenue

Mill Point Road

Hova Terrace

Way Rd

Westbury Rd

Berwick Street

Cargil Street

Gloucester St

Mackie Street

2

Meadowvale
Ave

Meadowvale
Shopping
Centre

Salisbury Avenue

Dyson

Darling Street

Brandon Street

Banksia Terrace

Hova Terrace

First Avenue

Second

Gwenyfred
Avenue Road

Lansdowne

Third Avenue

Fourth Avenue

Cargill Street

Mackie Street

McMaster Street

HAWTHORNE
PARK

Courthope St

King George St

Susan
St

Berwick Street

Roseberry Avenue

Dyson

Shaftesbury St

Canning Highway

Vista Street

Brandon Street

View Street

Fifth Ave

Sixth Avenue

Seventh Avenue

Eighth
Ave

George Street

Gwenyfred
Road

1

Ashstone Avenue

Jamieson Avenue

Broome

Pennington St

Collins

King St

Market St

Bright Street

Ankettel St

Pitt St

Ambon
St

Kernard Street

Lansdowne Road

Anketell Street

Lawler Street

Vista Street

King St

Market St

Street

MORRIS
MUNDY
RESERVOIR

Dyson

Oxford Street

Street

George Street

Kernard Street

Douglas Avenue

Arundel St

Carey St

KENSINGTON

140

Index

143

Insight Smart Guide: Perth
Compiled by: **Emma Green**
Proofread and indexed by: **Neil Titman**
Edited by: **Sarah Sweeney**

All photography by: **Glyn Genin/APA**
except: **Art Gallery of Western Australia**
76/77T; **The Birdgeman Art Library**
64L; **Coo-ee Picture Library** 64R;
iStockphoto.com 87C, 87B; **Paul
Kane/Getty Images** 5BR; **La Trobe Picture Collection, State Library of Victoria**
65R; **Mecca Cosmetica** 86/87T; **Mira-
max/Dimension Films/The Kobal Col-
lection/Penny Tweedie** 56/57T; **Newspix/News Ltd.** 26/27T, 54B,
62/63T, 74C, 82, 112/113T; **Newspix
/Rex Features** 56B; **Pension of Perth**
62/63B; **Perth International Arts Festival** 54/55T; **Perth Theatre Company**
116/117(all); **Rise** 84/85T; **Rottnest
Channel Swim Association** 114/115T;
West Australian Ballet 83B; **Western
Australia Tourist Commission** 80B,
128; **Michael Willis/Alamy** 40/41(all);
www.photovation.com.au 36/37T

Picture Manager: **Steven Lawrence**
Maps: **James Macdonald and
Encompass Graphics**
Series Concept: **Maria Lord**
Series Editor: **Jason Mitchell**

First Edition 2008
© 2008 Apa Publications GmbH & Co. Verlag KG Singapore Branch, Singapore.
Printed in Singapore by Insight Print
Services (Pte) Ltd

Worldwide distribution enquiries:
**Apa Publications GmbH & Co. Verlag KG
(Singapore Branch)**
38 Joo Koon Road,
Singapore 628990;
tel: (65) 6865 1600;
fax: (65) 6861 6438

Distributed in the UK and Ireland by:
GeoCenter International Ltd
Meridian House, Churchill Way West,
Basingstoke, Hampshire RG21 6YR;
tel: (44 1256) 817 987;
fax: (44 1256) 817 988

Distributed in the United States by:
Langenscheidt Publishers, Inc.
36–36 33rd Street 4th Floor, Long Island
City, New York 11106; tel: (1 718) 784
0055; fax: (1 718) 784 0640l

Contacting the Editors
We would appreciate it if readers would alert
us to errors or outdated information by
writing to:
Apa Publications, PO Box 7910, London SE1
1WE, UK; fax: (44 20) 7403 0290;
e-mail: insight@apaguide.co.uk

Around Perth

0   30 km

0   20 miles

N

SWAN VALLEY AND THE PERTH HILLS
pages 22–23

COTTESLOE, CLAREMONT, SWANBOURNE AND SCARBOROUGH
pages 20–21

FREMANTLE

See inset

Rottnest Island

Scarborough Beach
Scarborough
Swanbourne
Claremont
Cottesloe

Darling Range

Konnongorring
Lake Koombekine
Oak Park
Botherling
Nambling
Berring
Goomalling
Southern Brook
Meckering
Grass Valley
Mottlock
Quellington
Malebelling
Greenhills
Reading Hill 387
St Pauls Church
Beverley
Marlee
St Peters Church
Dale Bridge
Avon
Avondale Discovery
Gwambygine Pool
Talbot Brook
York
Mt Talbot
Burges
Spencers Brook
Muresk
Northam
Clackline
Bakers Hill
Wooroloo
The Lakes
Chidlow
Mundaring
Mundaring Weir Hotel
Helena
Mt Dale

Konnongorring
Mortlock North
Burabadji
Karrandgin
Hulongine
Jennacubbine
Yarramony
Jennapullin
Wongamine
Irishtown
Toodyay
Dewars Pool
Avon Valley Nat Park
Cartref Park
Chittering Valley
Lake Chittering
Chittering
Bindoon
Bullsbrook
Muchea
Upper Swan
Wanneroo
Wooroloo
Woodbridge
Midland
Guildford
Swan
Kalamunda
Kalamunda Nat Park
Araluen
Brook
Pickering
Brook
Karragullen
Canning
Bickley

Botherling
Berring
Rossmore
Murberkin
Coondle
Clackline
Bejoording
Wattening
Wyening
Culham
Motha Falls
Walyunga Nat Park
Gidgegannup
John Forrest Nat Park
Greenmount Nat Park
Darlington
Glen Forrest
Mahogany Creek
Perth

Calingiri
Bolgart
New Norcia
Calcarra
Yerecoin
Carani
Gillingarra
Great Northern Hwy
Mogumber
Wannamal
Moore
Moore River Nat Park
Mooliabeenee
Gingin Brook East
Gingin
Barragoon Lake
Lake Pinjar
Guilderton
Wanneroo
Sorrento

Seabird
Cape Leschenault
Breton Bay
Ledge Point
Karakin Lakes
Lancelin
Lancelin Island
Edward Island
Dido Bay
Wreck Point
Two Rocks
Yanchep Beach
Yanchep
Yanchep National Park
Loch McNess
Neerabup National Park
Eglinton Rocks
Quinns Rocks

Brand Hwy

Blue Gum Camel Farm
Archery Park
Baylup

I N D I A N

O C E A N